MAKE IT HAPPEN!

Six Tools for Success

By
Edward D. Hess

"To do is to be."
– Socrates

"To be is to do."
– Plato

DEDICATION

To my wife Katherine for always encouraging me to try;
And to my daughter Jennifer for having the courage to try.

To My Teachers

Thank you.

Tom Aiello
David Bonderman
Professor Lyle Bourne
Brady
Stuart Carwile
Rick Chukas
Professor Richard D'Aveni
Professor Charlie Davison
Dr. Jerry Ellwell
John Franklin
Professor William Fulmer
Coach Charles Grisham
Jack Hess
Kim Hutchins
Professor Sidney Jourard
Coach Ed Kensler
Jack McGovern
Judge Harry J. Michael
Chip Newell
Dr. M. O'Neill
Justice Antonio Scalia
Alan Schwartz
Dr. Dick Waite
Ira Wender
Jack White

TABLE OF CONTENTS

T his book is based on over 25 years of experience as a lawyer and investment banker helping people achieve their business and personal goals. I want to share with you what I have learned about how successful businesses and successful people manage themselves for success.

This book is based on the premise that these six basic management tools:

1. **Strategic Fit;**
2. **Management By Objectives;**
3. **Chunking;**
4. **Risk/Reward Decision Making;**
5. **Mental Rehearsal; And**
6. **Mental Replay**

can be utilized by you to gain more control over your life and to increase your probability of achieving what is important to you.

Using these six tools daily will help you prioritize, focus, act, make decisions, and learn daily. Living an achieving life is a daily process and will become a daily habit.

This book is written for the tradeperson, craftsperson, professional, service worker, homemaker, and anyone who can read, who has common sense, and who wants to take more control over his or her life, and who wants to achieve more.

This book is not a business theory book. It is written for the non-business person. This book is not a fast read. It is part workbook. You will learn how to use those six tools by doing - by using them in your life. This book is neither a quick fix nor a one-time prescription. To be successful you have to learn to apply these six tools daily to your life. You have to do it and do it and do it, over and over, until they become part of you.

Let me emphasize. This is not a one-time event. Successful people analyze, prioritize, focus, make decisions, act, learn, re-analyze, prioritize, act, learn, and do it again and again and again.

You are probably asking yourself – can I do it? Make It Happen! Let me share with you one fundamental I have learned in 28 years of working with successful people:

A positive attitude and having the courage to try is far more important in achieving success than either intelligence or pedigree.

Throughout this book we will focus on:

1. What you want to achieve or accomplish with your life, and
2. How best to do it.

> **"Today is your day: Your mountain is waiting. So, get on your way!"**
> *- Dr. Seuss*

OUR GOALS:
To help you be more successful and to take more control over your life by using the six management tools daily in living your life.

OUR OBJECTIVES:
To help you:

1. Determine your goals;

2. Find your strategic fit;

3. Play to your strengths;

4. Prioritize your actions;

5. Chunk your action plan into bite-size, achievable parts;

6. Focus your time and energy;

7. Measure your progress;

8. Make better decisions;

9. Better prepare to act; and

10. Learn from your actions.

Chapter One **A Proactive Can-Do Attitude**

1. Change is the New Constant

We live in a world characterized by fast-paced change. Change occurs more frequently and at a faster pace. More information is available to more people quicker through the Internet, Federal Express, the TV, and other mediums of communication.

As a result of this fast-paced change, reaction times are shorter; strategic or competitive advantages are shorter. We are bombarded by more people wanting more and quicker answers.

The world is a smaller place. The world's economies are linked together. No one's job or employer is isolated or protected from global events or global competition. The result is more job insecurity.

The free and fast flow of information produces more choices for more people. Some people view this as information overload and added stress.

Knowledge is now available to anyone, anywhere, anytime so long as you have access to a computer and a modem.

Jobs are being transformed by the global economy. More people are working in lower paying service jobs. More couples have to have both spouses working to make ends meet. Some people have to work more than one job.

The fundamental contract of lifetime employment between employer and employee is a thing of the past. No longer can you rely on the fact that good work will insure that you have a specific job. You can no longer rely on your employer to take care of you. Uncertainty, anxiety, and concern about job security are the new predominant feelings.

An environment which changes often, quickly, and along multiple dimensions is called a hyper-change environment. This is the era we live in. And I'm sorry to say that life will become more, not less, hectic; change is the new constant. We must all learn to adapt our professional and personal lives to this change. We must accept and embrace change.

A constantly changing environment is scary. Once you feel you have your life under control, something happens to throw it out of kilter again. Change, ambiguity, and instability. How does one cope in this new environment?

> **"There is nothing permanent except change."**
>
> *- Heraclitus*

2. You Are Your Answer

This environment of hyper-change, globalization, more information, more choices, and job insecurity requires us to take more ownership of our lives.

Your only real security is your skills, your values, and your ability to learn.

Even in a world of hyper-change, basic human nature has not changed. We are all primarily concerned about physical safety, shelter, food, economic security, a better life for our children, living a meaningful life, and being loved and appreciated by others.

Unless you accept ownership and responsibility for your life, you will not achieve your goals. No one is going to take care of you or do it for you. Yes, loved ones and friends will help; but they cannot do it for you. You are your answer.

> **"Nothing can bring you peace but yourself."**
> *- Ralph Waldo Emerson*

> **"Happiness depends upon ourselves."**
> *- Aristotle*

> **"The man who makes everything that leads to happiness depend upon himself and not upon other men, has adapted the best plan for living happily."**
> *- Plato*

3. You Have Two Basic Lifestyle Choices

You have two fundamentally different ways to respond to this new hyper-change environment:

Either

A Proactive Can-Do Approach

OR

A Reactive Approach

It is pretty simple. You can be either a proactive, can-do person and try to make things happen which you value or want; or you can be a reactive person and let things happen to you. For you to achieve more and have more control over your life, you have to be mostly a proactive, can-do person.

What is a proactive, can-do life approach?
A proactive, can-do life approach means that you:
• Accept responsibility for your life;
• Take ownership of your life;
• Adopt a positive "Can-Do" attitude;
• Attack life daily and go after what is important to you;
• Make something happen - be an impact player;
• Structure your life so that it represents those values which are most important to you.

What is a reactive approach?
A reactive approach means that you:
• Always accept whatever life has dealt you, believing that is your fate;
• Hope your life will get better;
• Passively make the best out of whatever comes your way;
• Believe that other people are to blame for your circumstances;
• Doubt that you can change your situation;
• Do not look forward to each day and its challenges; and
• Accept a martyr or "luck-of-the-draw" attitude.

Your attitude is crucial. A can-do, make-something-happen attitude comes from having self-confidence and believing in something that is important to you. Having values and faith are essential. Our goal is to learn tools which will help you be more successful in your work and personal lives.

Achieving more will give you more self-confidence. This will create a more positive attitude and a willingness to be more proactive.

"People are always blaming their circumstances for what they are. The people who get on in this world are those who get up and look for circumstances they want, and if they can't find them, make them."
- George Bernard Shaw

"A life of reaction is a life of slavery, intellectually and spiritually. One must fight for a life of action, not reaction."
- Rita Mae Brown

Chapter One Conclusions

1. Change is the new constant.

2. You are your answer.

3. You have to take responsibility for and ownership over your life.

4. Make It Happen!

5. You have two lifestyle choices:
A proactive can-do approach
OR
A reactive approach

6. A positive attitude is necessary for your success.

7. Faith and values are essential.

A proactive, can-do attitude is key to the approach of Make It Happen! Many people have a reactive attitude. That is okay. You can change your attitude if you want to. Let's first see where you are. Please check the box which best represents your feelings.

A. I believe I can make my life better.

☐ Yes   ☐ No

B. I look forward to each day as an opportunity.

☐ Yes   ☐ No

C. Each day is a burden to get through.

☐ Yes   ☐ No

D. I have too many things going against me.

☐ Yes   ☐ No

E. People look at me as a failure.

☐ Yes   ☐ No

F. You have to accept your role in life.

☐ Yes   ☐ No

G. Successful people are smarter than I am.

☐ Yes   ☐ No

H. I am scared of change.

☐ Yes   ☐ No

I. **I really cannot do much to improve my life.**
☐ Yes   ☐ No

J. **I generally wait to see what happens to me.**
☐ Yes   ☐ No

K. **I like to do things well.**
☐ Yes   ☐ No

L. **I am scared to try new things.**
☐ Yes   ☐ No

M. **Being proactive is hard work.**
☐ Yes   ☐ No

N. **I would like to have more control over my life.**
☐ Yes   ☐ No

O. **I would like to feel better about myself.**
☐ Yes   ☐ No

P. **I want to be successful and good at what I do.**
☐ Yes   ☐ No

Q. **I want to be a better person.**
☐ Yes   ☐ No

R. **I am a good person.**
☐ Yes   ☐ No

S. **It is hard for me to try new things.**
☐ Yes   ☐ No

Now, think about your answers.

Everybody wants to be a better person and to be good at what they do. We all want to make a better life for our children, and we all want our life to stand for something we believe in. Most people, however, do not know how to do it.

You can learn how to achieve more and how to have more control over your life. Learning how to do it is only part of the answer. Doing it successfully requires you to work on having a positive, can-do attitude, too.

A person with a proactive can-do attitude will have scored 100% by answering the questions above as follows:

A. Yes	F. No	K. Yes	P. Yes
B. Yes	G. No	L. No	Q. Yes
C. No	H. No	M. Yes	R. Yes
D. No	I. No	N. Yes	S. No
E. No	J. No	O. Yes	

> **"The greatest discovery of my generation is that man can alter his life by simply altering his attitude of mind."**
>
> *- William James*

> **"The last of the human freedoms: to choose one's attitude in any given set of circumstances, to choose one's own way."**
>
> *- Victor Frankel*

Each morning you have to put on your proactive, can-do attitude just like you put on your clothes. Ask yourself whether you're a "glass-is-half-full" kind of person, or whether you're a "glass-is-always-half-empty" kind of person.

Quit wasting time wishing for more or wishing you were different.

Wishin' Ain't Doin'

Make It Happen!
Start Today With A Positive Can-Do Attitude

Put these each on a 3x5 index card and place them on your bathroom mirror. Read them the first thing each morning.

Chapter Two Conclusions

(1) Start each day with a positive, can-do attitude.

(2) Be a can-do, proactive, make-something-happen person.

What have you learned in the first two chapters?

(1) _____

(2) _____

(3) _____

How can you feel more in control of your life?
How can you learn to accomplish more?

Successful people use 6 tools to better manage their lives for success. Let's learn about these tools now.

1. Strategic Fit - Finding Your Place

- What are you trying to accomplish?
- What are your goals?
- What are you good at?
- How can you maximize your chances of success?
- In what environment can you flourish?

Strategic fit is the process of aligning yourself and your environment so you can flourish. People do best when they place themselves in situations that are compatible with their values and where they have the opportunity to succeed by playing to their strengths.

To find your fit, you have to know yourself and.

1. Determine your goals - where you are going and what are you trying to accomplish?

2. Know your strengths so you can play to those strengths; and

3. Put yourself in situations which utilize your strengths, not your weaknesses.

Strategic fit is achieving the proper alignment between your goals, your values, your strengths, and your environment.

Strategic fit is actively structuring your life to play to your strengths; finding and creating the conditions which allow you to be you and flourish.

Strategic fit is playing to your strengths and putting yourself into situations which are more likely to help you accomplish your goals while minimizing your weaknesses. Strategic fit is making sure that your goals, abilities, skills, and environment are aligned, are compatible with each other, are working for you – that you have a good chance of accomplishing your goals.

> **"Happiness is when what you think, what you say, and what you do are in harmony."**
> *- Gandhi*

Once you have decided where you are going and what you want to do, how can you manage yourself to best achieve those results?

> **"What's important is finding what works for you."**
> *- Henry Moore*

Everyone has their own unique strategic fit. That is your uniqueness.

Successful people:
1. Know their goals;
2. Understand their strengths;
3. Play to their strengths; and
4. Put themselves into situations where they can flourish.

2. Management By Objectives

Management by Objectives is the process of learning to prioritize your actions – to focus your time and energy on your goals and to measure your results every day.

Management by Objectives is the daily self-discipline and management process which helps you move toward your goals. By doing so, you spend your time on what you have decided is important to you. You spend your time on accomplishing those daily tasks which will lead you toward your goals.

By using the Management by Objectives tool to manage how you spend your time, you will accept responsibility and ownership over your time and day. And as best as you can, you organize your day to accomplish your objectives for the day.

To manage your life by objectives, you set your objectives each day based on your goals and you work daily to achieve those objectives by moving toward your goals.

What is key is that you - not someone else - set your objectives. You decide what you can do each day to move toward your goals. You take responsibility for how you spend your time.

> **"Great things are not done by impulse, but by a series of small things brought together."**
>
> *- Vincent van Gogh*

Management by objectives requires that you:

• **Set objectives daily**

• **Prioritize daily**

• **Focus, focus, focus**

• **Measure your progress daily**

3. Chunking

Chunking is one of the most important tools to use to live a successful life. Chunking allows you to take a large task and break it down into bite-size chunks which are not as overwhelming as the large task. By chunking, you break down the task into its achievable component parts and take small steps toward success by accomplishing the chunks.

Break down your goals into logical step-by-step parts. Chunking is like a cake recipe. A recipe is all the small parts needing to be done to make a cake.

Chunks add up to objectives. I love the phrase, "Chunk it."

> **"Nothing is particularly hard if you divide it into small jobs."**
> *- Henry Ford*

4. Risk/Reward Decision Making

You have and will always have choices in your life. What to do? How to do it? With whom to do it? Move? Change jobs? Go back to school? Marry? Divorce? Change careers? How do businesses make decisions? What tools do they use?

Businesses make decisions in many different ways. Some are simple "gut" instinct decisions; some are analyzed in detail; some are computer modeled; some are debated with many people having input; but a common theme is:

Businesses weigh the risks and rewards, the pros and cons, and the upsides and downsides of most decisions.

Businesses try to take courses of action where the chances of success far exceed the chances of failure.

Businesses try to make decisions which maximize their future options and choices.

Businesses ask what can go right if I do action A; what can go wrong? How good is the right? How bad is the wrong? What is the chance of the wrong happening? Is the wrong easily fixable? What course of action maximizes my future flexibility? How can I keep my options open going forward?

Risk/reward decision-making is taking into account the potential positive and negative outcomes and implications. It is weighing the potential good versus the potential bad.

"Life is the sum of all your choices."
                                                    - Camus

5. Mental Rehearsal - The Inner Game

Successful people prepare for achieving their tasks. They think about how to accomplish the task at hand. They mentally rehearse the task, the phone call, or the meeting. They think about what they want to accomplish. They think about the objectives of the meeting, the call, the action.

Successful people think about the possible reactions before events occur. They play the game in their head before the actual game occurs. They close their eyes and see the act taking place. They mentally rehearse and prepare.

Successful people visualize in their mind the event and the other person's possible responses. They play the inner game before acting out the real game.

6. Mental Replay - The Rerun

The other side of mental rehearsal is mental replay. Once you have acted, stop and critique your performance. What could you have done better? What can you learn? What happened that you were not prepared for? What worked? What went wrong? How could you have done it better? What did you learn?

> **"The only man who makes no mistakes is the man who never does anything."**
>
> *- Eleanor Roosevelt*

You must learn to critique yourself fairly and frequently. That is how you learn. Review and learn.

What could you have done better?

> **"The quality of a person's life is in direct proportion to their commitment to excellence, regardless of their chosen field of endeavor."**
>
> *- Vince Lombardi*

You have to learn and improve. Why? Because your environment is changing. And to compete you have to continually be better. You learn by feedback from your environment – friends, employees, customers, and bosses.

Learning is how you get better.

The learning cycle is critical:

You act
▼
You get feedback
▼
You learn and get better
▼
You act again
▼
You get more feedback
▼
You learn more
▼
You get even better

Remember our goal:

To help you be more successful by using these six tools daily in your life.

Chapter Three Conclusions

(1) You are responsible for your life.

(2) You have to take ownership of your life.

(3) Make It Happen!

(4) How can I do it?

(5) By learning to use those 6 tools daily in your life.

I. STRATEGIC FIT

A. What am I trying to accomplish?

B. What are my strengths?

C. Play to my strengths.

D. Put myself in situations where I can flourish; align my values, strengths, and environment.

II. MANAGEMENT BY OBJECTIVES

A. Allocation of your time, energy, and resources to what is important to you;

B. Daily setting of your objectives;

C. Daily measurement of your progress;

D. Focus on accomplishing your objectives.

III. CHUNKING

A. Break down your goals and objectives into small bite-size chunks so you can focus on accomplishing small steps each day and week.

B. Chunks add up to objectives.

C. Daily/weekly accomplishments create good feelings and self-confidence and the enthusiasm to do more.

IV. RISK/REWARD DECISION MAKING

A. Every action has benefits and costs – pros and cons;
B. Think – what can go right? What can go wrong?
C. Weigh the potential results;
D. Maximize your future options;
E. Make decisions;
F. Act.

V. MENTAL REHEARSAL

A. Think about what you want to accomplish;
B. Visualize doing it;
C. Think about what can go wrong;
D. Think about and visualize the interactions;
E. Rehearse your words in your mind.

VI. MENTAL REPLAY

A. After each key task, review your actions;
B. Be critical but be fair;
C. Ask yourself what you could have done better;
D. Ask yourself what you have learned;
E. Ask yourself what you will do differently next time.

"Winning is not everything – but making the effort to win is."

- Vince Lombardi

Your Building Blocks to Success

Continual Learning
1. Act - Get Feedback - Learn - Act
2. Mental rehearsal to prepare to act
3. Mental replay to learn from your actions

Make Better Life Choices and Decisions
1. Risk/Reward Decision Making
2. Maximize future options

Manage Your Life to Achieve Your Objectives
1. Prioritize
2. Focus, Focus, Focus
3. Break down your goals into bite-size chunks
4. Set daily goals and measure your progress daily
5. Be proactive and make something happen

Find Your Strategic Fit
1. Determine your goals
2. Take into account your strengths, weaknesses, and environment
3. Play to your strengths
4. Have a positive, can-do attitude
5. Be proactive - Make something happen

Your Workspace

The first step in managing your life for success is determining what you want to accomplish. What are your goals? Your goals will define success for you. You have to find your strategic fit - the alignment of your values, strengths, and environment so you can flourish and achieve your goals. What is your destination and what road will you take? We only have so many hours a day, so many days in our life – so what do we focus on – what do we spend our time doing?

Businesses create mission statements to communicate to their employees, owners, and customers the purposes of why they exist. Remember the TV show, Mission Impossible? The show started by stating the team's mission – what they were going to try to do.

In a hyper-changing world, it is especially important that you be anchored by your life's goals and values. As you are bombarded by choices, change, and challenges, your goals and values will allow you to make choices which you hope will move you toward your goals. They are your guideposts.

Your goals and values are your lighthouse – a beacon to you. They are your reason for living – they are what are important to you.

Your goals and values define you and your life. They answer the question – "What will my life stand for?"

Strategic fit is finding your place – where your values are affirmed – where you can flourish.

I cannot stress values enough. They are the overriding definers of your life. You need to believe in something more than material success – something more important than you - something everlasting.

Most people define success in economic or material ways. Based on my life experiences, I have never met a happy or satisfied person whose definition of success was totally dictated by how much money he or she made.

No, we all are alike in that we are looking for more - to do more - to make a difference - to be loved and appreciated - to belong to something bigger than ourselves - to have immortality - to be thought of as a good person.

It has helped me to think of my life as having different components, all of which play a role in defining me and determining my goals.

Think about your goals and objectives in each of these areas:

- Work
- Family
- Play
- Relationships
- Spirituality
- Community

Let's explore together. Please write down your answers in the space provided after each question.

1. How do you define success for yourself?

_____
_____
_____
_____

2. At the end of your life, what do you want your life to have stood for?

_____
_____
_____
_____

3. At your funeral, how do you want to be remembered?

_____
_____
_____
_____

4. What accomplishments would make you feel good about yourself?

_____
_____
_____
_____

5. What are your hopes and dreams?

_____
_____
_____
_____

6. What tasks or activities give you the most inner joy or happiness?

_____

_____

_____

_____

7. When do you feel at peace with yourself?

_____

_____

_____

_____

8. What three words best define you as a person?

(a) _____

(b) _____

(c) _____

9. What causes you the most concern or worry?

_____

_____

_____

_____

10. What scares you about life?

_____

_____

_____

_____

11. What do you worry about?

_____

_____

_____

_____

12. **What are the three most important things in your life?**

_____

_____

_____

_____

13. **If you could be granted one wish, what would it be?**

_____

_____

_____

_____

14. **If you could be someone else, who would you be?**

_____

_____

_____

_____

15. **Why?**

_____

_____

_____

_____

16. **If you could live anywhere in the world, where would you live?**

_____

_____

_____

_____

17. Why?

_____

_____

_____

_____

18. If you received $50,000 tomorrow, what would you do with it?

_____

_____

_____

_____

19. Why?

_____

_____

_____

_____

20. What are you willing to die for?

_____

_____

_____

_____

21. Why do you get up in the morning?

_____

_____

_____

_____

22. What motivates you? What makes you tick?

_____

_____

_____

_____

As you thought about your answers, you probably thought on two very different levels.

Level 1 – Economic well-being, food, housing, physical safety, and health.

Level 2 – Values such as love, being appreciated, integrity, spirituality, respect, dignity, and meaning.

That is good!

You should constantly evaluate yourself – your life – on both levels. True inner peace, happiness, and joy comes from Level 2 values.

Abraham Maslow, a renowned authority of human behavior, created a pyramid of human needs and goals and stated that humans had different needs at any given time, depending on where they were on the hierarchy.

Maslow stated that you are motivated to meet your needs at your level of the pyramid before you can move up to a higher level of need. That is, before you can meet your esteem needs, you must have satisfied your love, safety, and physiological needs.

MASLOW'S HIERARCHY OF NEEDS

I studied Maslow 33 years ago and his view of the hierarchy of needs has stood my test of time. It has helped me understand people and organizations better and to help them focus on the right level of goal setting.

Understanding where you are on the pyramid helps you focus and prioritize your goals. Most happy people never achieve their goals - they are living a process of constantly improving, growing, achieving different objectives in different areas of their lives. You see, it is the process that is most important. It is how you play the game of life each day.

To be human is to dream for more in your life; to be alive is to strive for more; to compete in the game of life is to do your best every day. The end game is how you play the game.

Where do you fit on Maslow's hierarchy of needs? Does it help you understand yourself better? Does it help you prioritize your needs or goals? Does it help you order your life?

Let's compartmentalize your life into its different parts:

(a) Work
(b) Family
(c) Relationships (friends)
(d) Play (leisure, hobbies)
(e) Community
(f) Spirituality

Now, think about your answers to the previous questions; think about Maslow's Hierarchy; and think about the six component parts of your life.

Please understand why this part is so important. It is intended to help you determine, evaluate, reevaluate or better understand where you are going with your life now – here in this moment. Yes, your goals may change, but where you are going now determines how you spend your time, energy, money, today.

Your goals are the basic building blocks, the guideposts for your life's decisions.

Thus, the first step is "Where do you want to go with your life?" The second step is asking "Are you living your life so as to get there?"

You cannot manage your life better or get more control over your life unless you know where you are going.

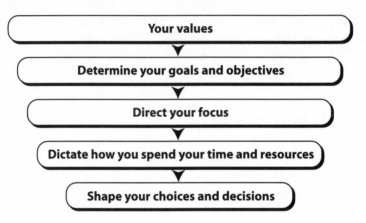

Successful people are not smarter than you or better than you. Mostly they are more focused and disciplined. They waste less time. They are intensely focused on obtaining their goals.

Let's try again.

First – list the three most important things, values, or principles in your life.

1. _____

_____

2. _____

_____

3. _____

_____

Make it Happen!

Now – look at each of these three most important things and be more specific about each one.

Explain what is really important about each; what really matters to you about each of the three.

1. _____

   a. _____

      _____

      _____

   b. _____

      _____

      _____

   c. _____

      _____

      _____

2. _____

   a. _____

      _____

      _____

   b. _____

      _____

      _____

   c. _____

      _____

      _____

3. _____
   a. _____

      _____

      _____

   b. _____

      _____

      _____

   c. _____

      _____

      _____

Okay. This is good. You are making progress.
Remember, Make It Happen!

Now, let's think about your six life compartments – work, family, relationships, play, community, and spirituality. In each compartment list the three most important things you want to do or accomplish. If you have more than three or less than three in any one compartment, that is okay. Adjust and adapt the exercise to you and your goals.

In thinking about the six areas of your life, focus on:
- What gives you joy or good feelings in each area?
- What makes you feel proud of yourself?
- When are you the most happy, the most at peace with yourself?
- What is fun for you?
- What is meaningful?
- What do you want to accomplish?

Your Work Life
1. _____
2. _____
3. _____

Your Family Life
1. _____
2. _____
3. _____

Your Relationships
1. _____
2. _____
3. _____

Your Play
1. _____
2. _____
3. _____

Your Community
1. _____
2. _____
3. _____

Your Spiritual Life
1. _____
2. _____
3. _____

You now should have a beginning list of potential goals and objectives – things you value. Good. You have started your process. You have accomplished the first step. You have started trying to figure out what you want to do with your life.

Understand that you will, and you should, review, revise, and reevaluate your goals and objectives as you experience life, as you learn, as you age, as you accomplish some of your objectives.

Prioritization

On any given day, you cannot try to accomplish all or even most of your goals and objectives. That does not mean they are not important. It is just that you have to prioritize your goals and objectives so that on a daily basis you can focus on the most important ones. How can you do this?

First – your three most important life's goals are your guideposts. Second, in each area of your life, you have goals. Prioritize them so you have a list of what is important to you. Make your list.

My goals are:

1. _____

2. _____

3. _____

4. _____

5. _____

6. _____

7. _____

The key is to do something each day to move in the right direction – toward your goals. Time is precious. Your time is limited and valuable. What you should have learned by now is that you are defined by how you spend your time. You are what you do. You must choose to spend your time wisely, to do what you want to do in order to achieve those goals which affirm your values.

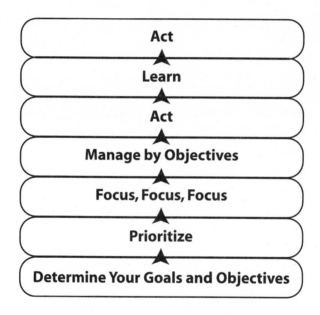

What I hope you learned here is a process of how to think about and determine what is important to you – a framework for you to continually paint your own picture. As your life changes, you will change, and what is important to you may also change.

> **"The only happy people I know are the ones who are working well at something they consider important."**
> - *Abraham Maslow on Management (p.9)*

Chapter Four Conclusions

Your Name: _____

Date: _____

The Most Important Overriding Things or Values in My Life Are:

1. _____

2. _____

3. _____

My Priorities – Six Life Compartments:

1. _____

2. _____

3. _____

4. _____

5. _____

6. _____

My Goals and Objectives For the Six Compartments:

1. _____

    a. _____

    b. _____

    c. _____

2. _____

    a. _____

    b. _____

    c. _____

3. _____

    a. _____

    b. _____

    c. _____

4. _____

    a. _____

    b. _____

    c. _____

5. _____

    a. _____

    b. _____

    c. _____

6. _____

    a. _____

    b. _____

    c. _____

<u>Your Workspace</u>

Your Strengths and Weaknesses

I n Chapter Four, you set forth your goals and objectives –
where you want to go. The second step in finding your
strategic fit is to objectively determine your strengths and
weaknesses from a personal viewpoint and from a work
viewpoint. When you understand your strengths and weaknesses
then you can realistically determine what you need to do in
order to accomplish your goals – what you need to improve –
what you need to learn.

Remember, successful people find their strategic fit - their
"place." They align their life so that they are playing to their
strengths in moving toward their goals. They find this fit or place
by understanding their strengths, gifts, and best attributes. They
increase their chance of success by finding harmony between their
strengths and their goals.

The goal here is to play to your strengths and have consistency
and compatibility between your strengths and your goals.
Strategic fit is aligning your goals, strengths, and environment so
they affirm your values and increase your ability to achieve your
goals.

Example – If one of your work goals is to become a manager in
your company and that requires computer skills but you have no
computer skills, then you know what you need to do. Learn
computer skills.

Example – If one of your life's goals is to work in your church 20
hours a week and help the elderly, but your job requires that you
travel for extended periods of time, then you have a problem to
solve. Do you defer your goal, change jobs, or change your goal?

Successful businesses "play to their strengths," their competencies, their areas of excellence. They work hard at being good at specific tasks, skills, or activities. They minimize their weaknesses by recognizing them, improving them, if possible, and by not putting themselves into positions where their weaknesses are the key determining factors of success.

Know who you are, know what you are good at, know what you enjoy, and do that.

> **"What's important is finding what works for you."**
> *- Henry Moore*

> **"A musician must make music, and an artist must paint; a poet must write if he is ultimately at peace with himself."**
> *- Abraham Maslow*

> **"Happiness is when what you think, what you say, and what you do are in harmony."**
> *- Gandhi*

I love that Gandhi quote. Harmony is when you think, do and say consistent things. Harmony is alignment. Harmony is being at peace with oneself.

To find your strategic fit, you should find a job or profession that allows you to play to your strengths, find activities outside of work that fulfill your personal needs, and create your own environment that will allow you to flourish. This is taking ownership over your life.

I will give you a personal example to illustrate what I mean. I have always loved country music. A dream of mine was to write country music songs. However, I have learned I am awful at hearing music and understanding rhythm. I cannot dance well even after a lot of lessons and practice. Music does not flow inside of me. Well, if I am ever going to be involved in the country music industry, I have to be realistic; I have to understand my strengths and my weaknesses. It will not be as a writer, singer, or performer, but more likely as a business advisor.

Your Strengths/Weaknesses

Again, it would be helpful to write down your answers to the following questions. Be honest with yourself and please think before you write.

1. What do you really enjoy doing? Tasks?

_____

_____

_____

_____

2. What do people say you are good at?

_____

_____

_____

_____

3. What do you feel you are bad at?

_____

_____

_____

_____

4. What tasks do you not enjoy doing?

_____

_____

_____

_____

5. What do you find hard to do?

_____

_____

_____

_____

6. What feedback have you received on your job evaluations as to your strengths and weaknesses?

_____

_____

_____

_____

7. **What have your colleagues and friends said are your strengths?**

_____

_____

_____

_____

8. **Do you like working with numbers? Why?**

_____

_____

_____

_____

9. **Do you like working with ideas or concepts? Why?**

_____

_____

_____

_____

10. **Do you like to write? Why?**

_____

_____

_____

_____

11. Do you like to speak in public? Why?

_____

_____

_____

_____

12. Do you like to work with your hands? Why?

_____

_____

_____

_____

13. Do you like to be indoors? Why?

_____

_____

_____

_____

14. Do you like to be outdoors? Why?

_____

_____

_____

_____

15. Do you like working with people? Why?

_____

_____

_____

_____

16. Do you like being around animals? Why?

_____

_____

_____

_____

17. Do you like working with machines? Why?

_____

_____

_____

_____

18. Do you like to do similar things each day? Why?

_____

_____

_____

_____

19. Do you like doing different things each day? Why?

_____

_____

_____

_____

20. Do you like playing analytical games like chess, checkers, bridge? Why?

_____

_____

_____

_____

21. Do you like to be alone often? Why?

_____

_____

_____

_____

22. Do you like to be part of a team? Why?

_____

_____

_____

_____

23. Are you a good salesperson?

_____

_____

_____

_____

24. Do you like working with the public? Why?

_____

_____

_____

_____

25. Do you like helping people? Why?

_____

_____

_____

_____

26. Do you enjoy social causes? Why?

_____

_____

_____

_____

27. Do people like you? Why?

_____

_____

_____

_____

28. How do you best learn? By reading? By watching? By listening? By hands-on?

_____

_____

_____

_____

29. Do you like computers?

_____

_____

_____

_____

30. What is the most fun thing you do during your job now?

_____

_____

_____

_____

31. What is the most difficult thing you do on your job now? Why?

_____

_____

_____

_____

32. What is your dream job? Why?

_____

_____

_____

_____

33. If you were given an amount of money equal to one times your annual salary, what would you do concerning your job?

_____

_____

_____

_____

34. What skills do you need to learn to advance in your job?

_____

_____

_____

_____

35. What do you really like to do in your spare time?

_____

_____

_____

_____

36. Do you enjoy your hobbies more than your job? Why?

_____

_____

_____

_____

37. Are you outgoing? Shy? Quiet? Trusting of people? Afraid of people?

_____

_____

_____

_____

38. Do you like new challenges?

_____

_____

_____

_____

39. Do you look forward to each day?

_____

_____

_____

_____

40. Do you like doing the same task over and over?

_____

_____

_____

_____

41. Would you rather be very good at the task or learn a new task every few months?

_____

_____

_____

_____

42. When do you get bored?

_____

_____

_____

_____

43. Give yourself an A, B, C, or F grade in each of the following subjects:

Subject	Grade	Subject	Grade
Spelling	_____	Cooking/Baking	_____
Grammar	_____	Athletic Skills	_____
Writing	_____	Creativity	_____
Speaking	_____	Logical Thinking	_____
Multiplication/ Division	_____	Brainstorming	_____
		Crossword Puzzles	_____
Addition/Subtraction	_____	Checkers, Chess,	
Listening to People	_____	Jigsaw Puzzles	_____
Compromising with People	_____	Understanding People	_____
		Counseling People	_____
Trusting People	_____	Taking criticism,	
Using a Computer	_____	suggestions	_____
Foreign Languages	_____	Being Right	_____
Salesmanship	_____	Being Wrong	_____
Serving Others	_____	Gardening/Farming	_____
Household Skills (Electric, plumbing, carpentry)	_____	Playing with Children	_____

The above was not meant to be an aptitude test or an exhaustive list. I am happy to say that there are very good career counselors who can help you if you had an especially difficult time with this section. I encourage you to seek guidance in this area if you feel it would help you assess your strengths and weaknesses.

This part was meant to make you think about yourself, your interests, and your competencies.

We have begun the process of you understanding your strengths and weaknesses.

Now, let's continue our journey.

Based on your answers to all of the above questions and after thinking about yourself, please write down your seven strengths and your seven weaknesses as a person. The strengths and weaknesses you list should apply to both your work and non-work life.

My Strengths   ## My Weaknesses

1.   1.

2.   2.

3.   3.

4.   4.

5.   5.

6.   6.

7.   7.

Now, let's see how others view us. Ask your two best friends, one at work and one personal friend, to give you a list of your strengths and weaknesses and tell them that you need their honest answers in order for this task to be effective and meaningful.

Friend # 1

Strengths

1.
2.
3.
4.
5.
6.
7.

Weaknesses

1.
2.
3.
4.
5.
6.
7.

Friend # 2

Strengths

1.
2.
3.
4.
5.
6.
7.

Weaknesses

1.
2.
3.
4.
5.
6.
7.

Now, if you have job or work ratings or reviews, write down what feedback you have received from your employer as to your strengths and weaknesses.

Job Evaluations

My Strengths

1.
2.
3.
4.
5.
6.
7.

My Weaknesses

1.
2.
3.
4.
5.
6.
7.

Summary Chart of Strengths

My List	Friend #1	Friend #2	Job Evaluations
1)			
2)			
3)			
4)			
5)			
6)			
7)			

Think about your list and the feedback from friends and work. Now, after thinking about it for a while and being open to their views, let's re-do your list.

My Revised Strengths

1. _____

2. _____

3. _____

4. _____

5. _____

6. _____

7. _____

Now, let's do the same thing for your weaknesses.

Summary Chart of Weaknesses

My List	Friend #1	Friend #2	Job Evaluations
1)			
2)			
3)			
4)			
5)			
6)			
7)			

Again, think about your list and the feedback from friends and work. Now, after thinking about it for a while and being open to their views, let's re-do your list of weaknesses.

My Revised Weaknesses

1. _____
2. _____
3. _____
4. _____
5. _____
6. _____
7. _____

Remember our goals: to play to our strengths, to emphasize them by making choices that affirm our strengths while working to minimize the impact of our weaknesses. We want to find our strategic fit and alignment. We want to live a harmonious life where our values, actions, and goals are aligned and play to our strengths. We want goals which we can achieve and that are compatible with who we are. We want to put ourselves in places, environments, jobs, that affirm our values and allow us to grow and achieve by playing to your strengths.

Chapter Five Conclusions

My strengths are (both personal and job related):

1. _____
2. _____
3. _____
4. _____
5. _____
6. _____
7. _____

My weaknesses are (both personal and job related):

1. _____
2. _____
3. _____
4. _____
5. _____
6. _____
7. _____

The next task will be to compare your strengths and weaknesses to your goals and objectives. Can you accomplish your goals? Do they play to your strengths? Are you realistic about who you are and what you want to do?

> **"A musician must make music, and an artist must paint; a poet must write if he is ultimately at peace with himself."**
>
> *- Abraham Maslow*

Make it Happen!

Your Workspace

Do Your Goals Fit With Your Strengths?

Now let's see if your strengths fit with your work, family, relationship, play, community, and spiritual goals.

Let's stop a minute and think. One of the concepts we have learned is that successful people play to their strengths.

Strategic fit is the process of aligning what you want to accomplish with what you are capable of accomplishing.

Alignment is the process of finding your FIT – how do your goals FIT with your strengths? It makes sense to choose goals that are important to you and for which you have or can obtain the necessary skills which are needed to accomplish those goals.

Your strengths and weaknesses are relevant in terms of whether they will help or hinder you in achieving your goals.

Too many people do not accept who they are and what they are good at and are frustrated by repeated mediocre performances. Everyone has strengths, skills, and natural abilities. Understand yours; be you; and let yourself flourish!

Please go back to pages 54-56 and your lists of objectives and goals for each of the six compartments of your life. Think about your goals and for each goal write down the critical or important or necessary skills, attributes, or qualities which you must have to accomplish the goal.

WORK GOALS

Work Goal #1

Necessary Skills/Attributes/
Qualities to Accomplish My
Goals and Objectives

_____	_____
_____	_____
_____	_____
_____	_____

WORK GOALS

Work Goal #2

Necessary Skills/Attributes/
Qualities to Accomplish My
Goals and Objectives

_____

_____

_____

_____

WORK GOALS

Work Goal #3   Necessary Skills/Attributes/
                                      Qualities to Accomplish My
                                      Goals and Objectives

_____   _____

_____   _____

_____   _____

_____   _____

                                      _____

                                      _____

                                      _____

                                      _____

                                      _____

                                      _____

                                      _____

                                      _____

                                      _____

                                      _____

                                      _____

                                      _____

                                      _____

                                      _____

FAMILY GOALS

Family Goal # 1

Necessary Skills/Attributes/
Qualities to Accomplish My
Goals and Objectives

_____

_____

_____

_____

_____

_____

_____

_____

_____

_____

_____

_____

_____

_____

_____

_____

_____

_____

_____

_____

_____

_____

_____

_____

_____

FAMILY GOALS

Family Goal # 2

Necessary Skills/Attributes/
Qualities to Accomplish My
Goals and Objectives

_____   _____

_____   _____

_____   _____

_____   _____

_____

_____

_____

_____

_____

_____

_____

_____

_____

_____

_____

_____

_____

FAMILY GOALS

Family Goal #3

Necessary Skills/Attributes/
Qualities to Accomplish My
Goals and Objectives

_____

_____

_____

_____

_____

_____

_____

_____

_____

_____

_____

_____

_____

_____

_____

_____

_____

_____

_____

_____

_____

_____

PLAY GOALS

Play Goal #1

Necessary Skills/Attributes/
Qualities to Accomplish My
Goals and Objectives

_____

_____

_____

_____

_____

_____

_____

_____

_____

_____

_____

_____

_____

_____

_____

_____

_____

_____

_____

_____

_____

_____

PLAY GOALS

Play Goal #2

Necessary Skills/Attributes/
Qualities to Accomplish My
Goals and Objectives

_____   _____

_____   _____

_____   _____

_____   _____

                                 _____

                                 _____

                                 _____

                                 _____

                                 _____

                                 _____

                                 _____

                                 _____

                                 _____

                                 _____

                                 _____

                                 _____

PLAY GOALS

Play Goal #3

Necessary Skills/Attributes/
Qualities to Accomplish My
Goals and Objectives

_____

_____

_____

_____

RELATIONSHIP GOALS

Relationship Goal #1

Necessary Skills/Attributes/
Qualities to Accomplish My
Goals and Objectives

_____   _____

_____   _____

_____   _____

_____   _____

_____

_____

_____

_____

_____

_____

_____

_____

_____

_____

_____

_____

RELATIONSHIP GOALS

Relationship Goal #2

Necessary Skills/Attributes/
Qualities to Accomplish My
Goals and Objectives

_____

_____

_____

_____

RELATIONSHIP GOALS

Relationship Goal #3

Necessary Skills/Attributes/
Qualities to Accomplish My
Goals and Objectives

_____

_____

_____

_____

_____

_____

_____

_____

_____

_____

_____

_____

_____

_____

_____

_____

_____

_____

_____

_____

_____

_____

_____

_____

COMMUNITY GOALS

Community Goal #1

Necessary Skills/Attributes/
Qualities to Accomplish My
Goals and Objectives

_____

_____

_____

_____

_____

_____

_____

_____

_____

_____

_____

_____

_____

_____

_____

_____

_____

_____

_____

COMMUNITY GOALS

Community Goal #2

Necessary Skills/Attributes/
Qualities to Accomplish My
Goals and Objectives

_____

_____

_____

_____

<u>COMMUNITY GOALS</u>

Community Goal #3   Necessary Skills/Attributes/
                                     Qualities to Accomplish My
                                     Goals and Objectives

_____   _____

_____   _____

_____   _____

_____   _____

                                     _____

                                     _____

                                     _____

                                     _____

                                     _____

                                     _____

                                     _____

                                     _____

                                     _____

                                     _____

                                     _____

                                     _____

                                     _____

SPIRITUAL GOALS

Spiritual Goal #1

Necessary Skills/Attributes/
Qualities to Accomplish My
Goals and Objectives

_____

_____

_____

_____

SPIRITUAL GOALS

Spiritual Goal #2

Necessary Skills/Attributes/
Qualities to Accomplish My
Goals and Objectives

_____   _____

_____   _____

_____   _____

_____   _____

      _____

      _____

      _____

      _____

      _____

      _____

      _____

      _____

      _____

      _____

      _____

      _____

      _____

      _____

      _____

SPIRITUAL GOALS

Spiritual Goal #3

Necessary Skills/Attributes/
Qualities to Accomplish My
Goals and Objectives

_____

_____

_____

_____

Now, take your list of your strengths and weaknesses and compare them to the List of Necessary Skills/Attributes/Qualities to Accomplish My Goals and Objectives.

Evaluate each goal – what is necessary to accomplish it? Think about you – your strengths and weaknesses. **Do you have the necessary skills or the ability to learn or acquire the necessary skills?**

How do they match up? Do you have the necessary skills, attributes, or qualities? What do you need to learn? Which do you need to work on? Which goals and objectives now appear to be very difficult for you to achieve? Which need to be reevaluated?

Strategic fit is the process of finding the right fit for you – to do what plays to your strengths while minimizing the impact of your weaknesses.

Do you need to change some goals? If so, do it.

Do you need to reprioritize some goals? If so, do it.

Do you need to add new goals which better fit you? If so, do it.

Are you happy with your goals and objectives?

Do they fit you?

Are you playing to your strengths?

Think also about your job, your family life, how you spend your time daily.

Are you focusing on your goals daily?

Are you in positions or places which affirm you and your values and in which you can flourish?

What do you need to do to achieve more?

What do you need to do to be more successful?

What do you need to do to be happier?

Work Goals

I need to improve:

_____

_____

_____

I need to learn:

_____

_____

_____

I need to focus on:

_____

_____

_____

Family Goals

I need to improve:

_____

_____

_____

I need to learn:

_____

_____

_____

I need to focus on:

_____

_____

_____

Play Goals

I need to improve:

_____

_____

_____

I need to learn:

_____

_____

_____

I need to focus on:

_____

_____

_____

Relationship Goals

I need to improve:

_____

_____

_____

I need to learn:

_____

_____

_____

I need to focus on:

_____

_____

_____

Community Goals

I need to improve:

_____

_____

_____

I need to learn:

_____

_____

_____

I need to focus on:

_____

_____

_____

Spiritual Goals

I need to improve:

_____

_____

_____

I need to learn:

_____

_____

_____

I need to focus on:

_____

_____

_____

I want to come back to strategic fit.

Playing to strengths is what great sports teams do; or what great athletes do. Put yourself into positions and situations to use your best shot.

The most successful entrepreneurs and business people that I have known all know what they are good at and more importantly, what they are not good at.

Choose environments at work, at home, in your community, your social circle, and spiritual circle that fit you – that play to your strengths and that are consistent with your values and ideals. Find places where you are comfortable in terms of values and where you can flourish.

Choose friends and social relationships that are affirming of you and that help you grow and flourish. Seek out proactive, givers of life, not just takers

Strategic fit is the alignment of you, your goals, your strengths, and your environment so you can learn more, grow more, achieve more, and flourish!

Successful people are always tinkering, trying to improve, trying to learn more. Successful people do not achieve a goal and stop. Along the way their goals change. Successful people live a life of little achievements which add up or cumulate into bigger achievements. it is the process of how you live - how you play the game that gives you life's meaning.

Chapter Six Conclusions

1. You have reevaluated your goals and objectives in light of your strengths and weaknesses. You have modified or eliminated some goals; you may also have added some.

2. You have begun to think tactically, logically, about what you need to do to accomplish your goals.

3. You understand the necessity and importance of strategic fit – aligning your goals and objectives with your strengths.

4. You understand that successful businesses play to their strengths just as great athletes, artists, musicians, and dancers do.

5. You know you must seek environments, jobs, opportunities that allow you to play to your strengths.

6. People flourish in environments where they can play to their strengths and where their personal values are compatible with the environment.

7. Successful people enjoy what they are doing because they are good at it. It becomes natural after a while; it becomes part of them; it feels good to do something well.

8. Successful people develop a track record of success which gives them more self-confidence.

9. Playing to your strengths increases your chances of success.

10. Playing to your strengths will give you more self-confidence which leads to a proactive attitude.

Opportunities and Obstacles for Success in Your Environment

I n determining their goals, successful people not only assess their strengths and weaknesses, they also assess their external environment.

Your external environment includes your job world, your home life, your community; and your people environment. All of these environments must be taken into account in setting your goals and objectives, and in managing your life.

Remember, everything in your life – the people, your employer, the industry you work in, are changing all the time. Nothing remains stable; nothing remains the same. This constant change – some of it positive and some of it negative means that you cannot take anything for granted. You have to be aware – to hear, to feel, to sense changes in your environment and determine which are important to you and your goals.

Life is change. Sense it and respond to it. Hear it – Listen for it.

It is best to explain this by example.

Example #1: Work Life

Let's suppose that one of your goals was to progress at your job and be promoted to a supervisor. This would give you added responsibility and more pay which would allow you to save for your children's education.

Work Environment

Your company produces products in an industry where price competition is fierce. Many competitors have sought to reduce costs by either moving plants overseas or by automation. Your company's stock price is not doing well compared to its peers, its competitors.

"911 Alert"

You should sense that there is a good possibility that your company will have to do something to remain competitive. Options include closing U.S. plants, automating, or merging with a lower cost producer. But something will likely happen. Something is going to change.

What do you do?

Start thinking about alternatives for your career. Which of your skills are most marketable? Ask yourself the following questions: What skills should I learn to make myself more marketable? Should I budget more savings? What industry should I work in? Where is there a shortage of my skills? What can I do if my plant closes? What are my options? What can I do to maximize my options? Don't allow yourself to be shocked or surprised when change happens. Prepare as best you can for it.

Example #2: Play World

You have learned over the years that you get a lot of enjoyment out of water sports. It is fun, relaxing, and challenging. You would like to water-ski more and learn to sail. You love the feeling of freedom, joy, and the smell of water.

You currently live four hours away from the closest body of water. Your current environment - where you live - limits your ability to enjoy water sports to some weekends.

Alternatives

How important are your play goals as compared to your work, family, relationships, community, or spiritual goals?

What impact will moving have on your other goals? On your family?

There are no easy answers. Life is full of tradeoffs. You will learn about risk/reward decision making in Chapter Nine - every decision has pros and cons and each decision will ultimately impact other areas of your life.

Should you move closer to the water? Should you work in a water/sports-related business? Should you find another hobby which you can enjoy more often?

Example # 3: Spiritual World

One of your goals is to be more active in your church and work with the elderly. However, you live in an area where the only jobs are in the service industry or in one of the food processing plants. These jobs are low-paying jobs. You are a single parent and to make ends meet, you must work a full-time job and a part-time job. With your family responsibilities, you have little time for the church. This makes you feel guilty and unhappy.

Alternatives

Your environment and responsibilities limit your ability to do everything. Assuming your spiritual goals are very important to you, your options could include:

1. Moving to a better job market so you can make enough money with just one job;
2. Seeing if you could work part-time at the church for pay and quit your current part-time job; or
3. Find work in a service area where on a daily basis you can help the elderly.

Again, think about how you can structure your life to accomplish your most important goals. Understand that you can choose. You can change your environment if it impedes too many of your goals.

Managing your life is understanding that you can make choices, you can change your situation.

To manage your life for success means that you have to take responsibility for making your life better. Make It Happen!

Example #4: Family and Work

You work as an administrative assistant for a large company. Your family includes two young children ages two and four. You desperately want to spend more time with them while they are young. But you need additional income to help your spouse support your family.

Alternatives

What opportunities exist for you to work part-time from your home? Do you have the skills and equipment to work at home? Can you find a job at a daycare center where your children could also attend? Are there jobs where you could work three days a week for 12 hours a day? Again, what we are trying to do is to explore how to accomplish your goals within your environmental restraints.

We all have environmental restraints which we have to deal with.

It is okay to ask yourself how you can get more of what you want. Think creatively. You have options. Go for it – today.

Example #5:

You like working with your hands and with machinery. But to make more money at your current job or company you must move into a supervisory position. You are not good with people. You are a perfectionist and think most people just do barely enough to get by. You do not like listening to their excuses. Well, a supervisor's role is a people management role that requires patience, tolerance, and people skills.

You have a conflict between wanting to make more money and your strengths. You are good at what you do and you enjoy it. You will not be good at a supervisor's job unless you change and overcome some weaknesses. Change is hard. It is possible but it takes a lot of work.

Alternatives

1. Stay in your present position and work part-time outside your firm to make more money;
2. See if there is another job inside or outside your company which utilizes your machine skills and pays more money;
3. Accept the new job and ask your employer for training designed to improve your people skills.

How does your environment align or fit with your goals or objectives?

Now, for each of the six areas of your life (work, family, play, relationships, spirituality, and community), let us review your goals and objectives in light of your environment.

1. Your WORK goals and objectives are:

a. _____

b. _____

c. _____

d. _____

e. _____

f. _____

Your Environment

A. What in your environment will help you achieve these goals?

_____

_____

B. What in your environment will hinder you?

_____

_____

C. What in your environment can you change or improve to help you achieve your goals?

_____

_____

D. How can you minimize the negatives of your environment?

_____

_____

E. How can you exploit the positives in your environment?

_____

_____

2. Your FAMILY goals and objectives are:

a. _____

b. _____

c. _____

d. _____

e. _____

f. _____

Your Environment

A. What in your environment will help you achieve these goals?

_____

_____

B. What in your environment will hinder you?

_____

_____

C. What in your environment can you change or improve to help you achieve your goals?

_____

_____

D. How can you minimize the negatives of your environment?

_____

_____

E. How can you exploit the positives in your environment?

_____

_____

3. Your PLAY goals and objectives are:

a. _____

b. _____

c. _____

d. _____

e. _____

f. _____

Your Environment

A. What in your environment will help you achieve these goals?

_____

_____

_____

B. What in your environment will hinder you?

_____

_____

_____

C. What in your environment can you change or improve to help you achieve your goals?

_____

_____

_____

D. How can you minimize the negatives of your environment?

_____

_____

_____

E. How can you exploit the positives in your environment?

_____

_____

_____

4. Your RELATIONSHIPS goals and objectives are:

a. _____

b. _____

c. _____

d. _____

e. _____

f. _____

Your Environment

A. What in your environment will help you achieve these goals?

_____

_____

_____

B. What in your environment will hinder you?

_____

_____

_____

C. What in your environment can you change or improve to help you achieve your goals?

_____

_____

_____

D. How can you minimize the negatives of your environment?

_____

_____

_____

E. How can you exploit the positives in your environment?

_____

_____

_____

5. Your SPIRITUAL goals and objectives are:

a. _____

b. _____

c. _____

d. _____

e. _____

f. _____

Your Environment

A. What in your environment will help you achieve these goals?

_____

_____

B. What in your environment will hinder you?

_____

_____

C. What in your environment can you change or improve to help you achieve your goals?

_____

_____

D. How can you minimize the negatives of your environment?

_____

_____

E. How can you exploit the positives in your environment?

_____

_____

6. Your COMMUNITY goals and objectives are:

a. _____

b. _____

c. _____

d. _____

e. _____

f. _____

Your Environment

A. What in your environment will help you achieve these goals?

_____

_____

B. What in your environment will hinder you?

_____

_____

C. What in your environment can you change or improve to help you achieve your goals?

_____

_____

D. How can you minimize the negatives of your environment?

_____

_____

E. How can you exploit the positives in your environment?

_____

_____

In living a proactive life, it is important to remember your values. You are your values. Your are your actions. Act in a way that is consistent with your values – the values that you respect and cherish.

Act as if every action will be on the front page of your local newspaper.

Living a proactive life is being active and making things happen. However, it is not necessary to hurt others, belittle them, impede them, or step on anyone's back. Remember - How you get there is as important as getting there.

Chapter Seven Conclusions

1. Your external environment is a limitation on your ability to accomplish your goals. You have to deal with the reality of your circumstances.

2. Your environment consists of people at work, and at home; your friends, neighbors, family, etc. It is a changing environment in that events are happening daily in all of those people's lives. Understand that everything is changing. Nothing is stable.

3. Learn to see, hear, and feel trends, changes, and indications of change which may be important to you. Focus on hearing, seeing and feeling changes in your work environment, family environment, and relationship environments.

4. Try to structure your external environment to increase your chance of achieving your goals and objectives.

5. Sometimes you have to be willing to change something in your environment if it is destructive, unhealthy, or a significant negative in your life.

6. One's external environment must be taken into account in setting goals and objectives.

7. Let me stress one point here. Your external environment will always be limiting or constraining. The point is to take your environment into account in determining how to achieve your goals and objectives.

8. Too many people use their environmental constraints as an excuse not to try. Some people try to run away or leave their environment especially in situations where they have had a personal responsibility for creating that environment.

The first tool we learned is how to find your strategic fit. Aligning your values and goals to play to your strengths, taking into account your environment. Now we need to learn how to prioritize and focus on accomplishing your goals.

Successful businesses achieve superior performance by: (1) setting clear objectives (2) which can be clearly measured on an objective basis and (3) by rewarding people for accomplishing those objectives.

Management by Objectives ("MBO") requires one to prioritize, and focus one's efforts. It is a disciplinary process. How can you keep focused? How can you make the most of your time? How can you limit distractions?

To manage your life for success you have to prioritize and focus. You have set forth a list of your goals and objectives for your life and for the six compartments of your life – work, play, family, community, spiritual, and relationships. You listed your goals under each compartment. Then you prioritized the six compartments and goals.

In the strengths and weaknesses analyses you set forth the skills, attributes, or qualities which you either want to improve on, or acquire. You have a "to do" list.

You have your objectives. Now you need to set daily, weekly, and monthly goals which move you toward accomplishing what is important to you. Frequent movement toward your goals is the key.

Most people do not focus daily on accomplishing their goals. Most people get off the track too easily. Most people do not know how to manage their time effectively.

To manage your life for success you have to learn to say NO. You have to focus on doing what is important to you. You have to limit distractions and nonessential activities. Focus, focus, focus.

Focusing is understanding that you cannot do everything every day, but you can do what is most important to you. It is the hardest thing to learn - how to say no in order to protect yourself - your time - your focus.

Management by Objectives teaches you to:
1. Prioritize how you spend your time daily;
2. Prepare daily/weekly to do lists;
3. Focus your time and energy on accomplishing your to-do lists;
4. Check off your progress daily; and
5. Move toward your goals in a systematic way.

You have previously determined your goals and prioritized the six compartments of your life (work, family, play, relationships, spirituality, and community). So you know your objectives.

Setting objectives - your to-do list - should become a daily habit. Every day for 35 years I have made a to-do list. Each day I check off my accomplishments. These daily to-do's add up and culminate in bigger accomplished objectives.

To manage your life by setting objectives and creating your daily to-do lists requires you to learn about chunking.

Chunking is critical to making daily progress toward your goals - the objective.

Chunking

Chunking is the process of breaking down your goals or objectives into small component parts. Chunking creates small bite-size chunks or parts which can be accomplished daily. It allows you to make progress and measure your progress daily.

A good way to understand chunking is to compare it to a recipe. A recipe breaks down cooking a pie or cake, for example, into step-by-step component parts to be accomplished one at a time in a logical order. Chunking breaks down your goal into step-by-step logical parts.

Examples of Chunking:

1. Your goal is to become computer literate. To do so, you must complete at least these eight steps.

Bite-Size Chunks

1. Learn how to turn on the computer
2. Learn how to set up passwords
3. Learn how to set up files
4. Learn how to send e-mails
5. Learn how to prepare a written memo
6. Learn how to make corrections, deletions to your memo
7. Learn how to save documents and retrieve them
8. Learn how to use spreadsheets

2. You want to learn to play tennis.

Bite-Size Chunks

1. Learn how to hold a racket
2. Learn how to stand to receive the ball
3. Learn the basic rules
4. Learn how to hit the ball
5. Learn the forehand shot
6. Learn the backhand shot
7. Learn court strategy
8. Learn how to serve
9. Learn how to lob
10. Learn the drop shot
11. Learn how to put spin on the ball

"Great things are not done by impulse, but by a series of small things brought together."

- Vincent van Gogh

You cannot manage your life by objectives unless you chunk your goals and objectives into bite-size tasks, some of which can be accomplished daily and weekly.

If you do not chunk, you will be overwhelmed and you will have no way to achieve daily accomplishments which builds self-confidence and a positive can-do attitude.

"Little strokes fell great oaks."

- Benjamin Franklin

Successful people chunk their tasks and their time. They consciously set out to make step-by-step progress each day. They move the ball toward the goal line. Making progress generates self-confidence and positive self-regard. It feels good to make progress. Progress is success. Success is habit forming. Keep breaking down the tasks until they are small and manageable and understandable.

You cannot make the chunks too small.

Chunking also allows you to measure your progress. It allows you to set achievable, obtainable, reachable goals each day. Success is a daily habit. Chunks are your building blocks of success.

Now you have to take your goals and break them down one by one into their chunks – step-by-step acts needed to accomplish the goal.

GOAL # 1:

_____

Chunks for Goal #1

1. _____

2. _____

3. _____

4. _____

5. _____

6. _____

7. _____

GOAL # 2:

_____

Chunks for Goal #2

1. _____

2. _____

3. _____

4. _____

5. _____

6. _____

7. _____

GOAL # 3:

_____

Chunks for Goal #3

1. _____

2. _____

3. _____

4. _____

5. _____

6. _____

7. _____

GOAL # 4:

_____

Chunks for Goal #4
1. _____
2. _____
3. _____
4. _____
5. _____
6. _____
7. _____

GOAL # 5:

_____

Chunks for Goal #5
1. _____
2. _____
3. _____
4. _____
5. _____
6. _____
7. _____

GOAL # 6:

_____

Chunks for Goal #6
1. _____
2. _____
3. _____
4. _____
5. _____
6. _____
7. _____

GOAL # 7:

_____

Chunks for Goal #7
1. _____
2. _____
3. _____
4. _____
5. _____
6. _____
7. _____

Now you have prioritized your goals and objectives and you have your skill objectives. You have chunked them, broken them down into the step-by-step cookbook-like action steps.

"Nothing is particularly hard if you divide it into small jobs."

- Henry Ford

Now you are ready to set daily and weekly goals. What chunks do you plan to complete this week? This is managing yourself by objectives.

Your daily to-do lists should contain some of the chunks of your most important goals.

Managing your life by objectives includes:
1. Prioritizing your goals;
2. Breaking down your goals into bite-size, doable chunks;
3. Setting daily to-do lists to accomplish;
4. Doing it daily – making progress daily;
5. Checking off what you have accomplished daily;
6. Feeling good about making some progress each day; and
7. Making daily progress a habit!

MBO DAILY HELPERS

First: Priority Reminder Card
On a 3x5 index card write down your prioritized goals, objectives, and key skills which you need to acquire or improve on. Keep it with you at all times.

At breaks, or at lunch, on the train, or the bus, review the card. At a minimum, review this card once a day. Think about what you have done or need to do in order to make progress and move toward your goal.

Second: Daily To-Do List

Each day on a 3x5 card, write down in order of priority what chunks you need to do that day. Upon accomplishment, check off the chunk. Review this card at lunch and at night. If you did not accomplish a task, think about why. Carry that task over to the next day and do it first.

Let's set some objectives.

My to-do list for tomorrow is:

1. _____
2. _____
3. _____
4. _____
5. _____
6. _____

Now, on a 3x5 index card, write down your objectives for tomorrow:

Date: _____

Objectives:
1. _____
2. _____
3. _____
4. _____
5. _____
6. _____

Do your list each day. Check off your accomplishments. Do something each day that moves you toward – closer to – your goal. Act! Do it!

The key concepts here are:
1. Prioritization
2. Focus
3. Step-by-Step Progress
4. Measure Your Progress Daily
5. Daily Accomplishments Add Up to Progress

With the accomplishment of small tasks comes self-confidence and positive feelings about yourself which are fueled daily by your progress. This good feeling will lead you to do more. This is the habit of a successful, proactive, can-do lifestyle.

Let me talk about focus. Focus is the mental discipline to concentrate with all your energy on the task at hand. Focused people are more efficient and can accomplish more tasks and accomplish them faster. Focus is concentration. Focus is blocking out distracting thoughts or interruptions. Focus is what I call laser-like intensity of feeling all your concentration directed at the task.

Focus is saying NO to distractions. NO is protecting you and your time.

You will eventually revise your daily action lists to take into account what you need to do next to keep moving toward accomplishment of your goals, objectives and skill list.

Positive daily attitude + positive daily action = accomplishments

Each day you should feel good about your accomplishments and you should have resolve to correct or improve on your mistakes.

This daily feeling good about your accomplishments adds up emotionally, too. It should lead to you feeling better about yourself and having more self-confidence. This should lead to a more proactive life attitude – a can-do attitude; a make-something-happen attitude; an attack-life attitude.

Attitudes impact actions in that positive, enthusiastic people can impact their environment in more positive ways. Enthusiasm is catching. The goal is to be an impact player – someone who makes something happen every day.

> **"Mean to don't pick no cotton."**
> *- Anonymous*

> **"If you want to conquer fear, don't sit at home and think about it. Go out and get busy."**
> *- Dale Carnegie*

The key is to set your objectives and do it every day. Get it done. Eliminate the excuses.

Most people procrastinate too much. Most people are scared of failing. Most people are afraid to try. But by taking small steps you will learn to trust yourself and you will learn that a lot of life's successes come from having the courage to try every day.

Trust me. Try each day to do a small task which moves you toward a goal. Don't be deterred or sidetracked. Do something each day.

> **"Great things are not done by impulse, but by a series of small things brought together."**
> *- Vincent van Gogh*

> **"Life is like that; one stitch at a time taken patiently, and the pattern will come out all right, like embroidery."**
> *- Oliver Wendell Holmes*

Common Beginner's Problems With MBO

Now, it is common for people who adopt the MBO approach to get frustrated in the beginning because they feel they are not making enough progress.

1. **Impatience** – Progress is a daily, step-by-step process. ONE DAY AT A TIME. If you make your to-do lists and you accomplish most of the necessary steps or bit-size chunks, you are making progress. Don't be impatient. "Rome wasn't built in a day."

2. **Time Just Flies By** – Some people make up their lists and at the end of the day they have more undone items than they have accomplishments. This happens sometimes when uncontrollable events occur which need your attention. Priorities can unexpectedly change. But if it happens frequently, I suggest you keep track of how you spend your time for one week. Each day write down in 30-minute intervals what you did all day. Add up the time spent on each goal or objective or skill.

   Where are you spending nonproductive time? Where are you spending time that can be delegated to others? Where can you save time by being better organized? How can you free up some time?

   Protect your time. Don't waste your time. Time is your most precious resource.

3. **A.M. vs. P.M. Person** – A lot of people are more creative, productive, or efficient in the morning than the evening. For example, I am a morning person with 4:30 – 5:30 a.m. until 3:00 p.m. being my most creative and efficient time. 5:00 p.m. until 10:00 p.m. is my least efficient period of time.

   In structuring your day, try to take into account your peak efficiency time. If you are a morning person, and if you leave a lot of learning tasks until the evening, you will not be as efficient or successful. If that is the only time you have to learn during the week, use your weekend mornings very productively or efficiently.

4. **Interruptions and Distractions** – How many times have you been in the middle of something important to you and the phone rings, or your child comes in, or a friend interrupts you, or someone at work wants to talk. Unless it is very important, just clearly and politely ask if you can talk, see, or call them after you finish your task. Do not be distracted by unimportant interruptions. Control your time as best you can.

5. **Too Large Chunks** – Some people do not break their goals, objectives or skills down into small enough bites or chunks. As a result, their goal or objective looks overwhelming. You cannot chunk too small.

6. **"All Your Eggs in One Basket"** – Some people focus the vast majority of their time on one area of their life, for example, work. As a result, they emotionally become totally dependent on one area for their positive feelings about themselves. In today's volatile world, placing yourself in that situation could subject your life to many ups and downs beyond your control and limit your ability to find happiness and meaning. It is your conscious choice how to prioritize your six life compartments. I want you to understand not only the rewards but also to think about the downside or costs of only focusing on one area to the exclusion of all other areas.

7. **How Do You Learn Best?** – Some people learn best by reading, some by writing, some by hearing, some by watching demonstrations. Understand how you best learn. This is your most efficient and productive way to learn. Do it.

Like Nike said, "Just do it!"

What we are learning here is a process – a way to live life more fully, more proactively with you taking more control over what you do each day. Successful people are focused and disciplined. Happy people are productive and feel like they are more in control over their life because they are accomplishing things important to them.

You can be more successful and more happy. Take responsibility. Set your priorities and focus and do it. Today!

Have you made your to-do list?

Chapter Eight Conclusions

1. You have set your goals and objectives.

2. Chunking is: a step-by-step recipe approach for accomplishing each goal or objective.

3. Set daily and weekly goals.

4. Prioritize daily activities - make a daily to-do list.

5. Focus, Focus, Focus

6. Be disciplined.

7. Act daily.

8. Measure your progress daily.

9. Make a 3x5 card with a daily "to do" list.

10. Make It Happen! GET UP AND DO IT EACH DAY!

An attack life attitude is fun and inspirational. Be an impact player. Make something happen today. Make It Happen! I know you can! Just do it.

Your Workspace

L et's review. We have learned about:

1. Strategic fit – aligning your strengths and goals with your environment;
2. Playing to your strengths;
3. Setting daily priorities;
4. Chunking; and
5. Your daily to-do list - managing your life by objectives.

A proactive lifestyle by definition requires that you act and make something happen daily. Daily actions add up. A can-do lifestyle is a step-by-step process of acting daily and moving toward your goals and objectives.

The next step in the process is to learn some tools to help you decide what actions to take and how to make better choices. A proactive life – a "can-do" attitude – a make-something-happen lifestyle requires that you act and make choices, but not act blindly, stupidly, or without thinking about the consequences.

Making things happen – being an impact player will increase your choices as you move toward your goals. So you need to have tools to help you make better decisions. We are going to learn a decision process which, if used often and practiced, will become second nature.

Decision analysis – understanding the pros and cons of various alternatives and analyzing the upside (positive) and the downside (negatives) of various alternatives - is critical in minimizing major mistakes and maximizing movement toward your goals and objectives.

Daily, you make many decisions, some quickly and easily, some of minor consequence or impact, and some hard decisions with major downside or major upside impacts.

We all have many choices:
Do you stay in this job?
Do you move?
Do you change the kids' babysitter?
Do you date a twice-divorced man?
Do you stay home with the kids or go out?
Do you get pets?
Do you have more kids?
Do you date him or her?
Do you break up?
Do you leave him or her?
Do you confront an abusive partner or parent?
Which school should you choose?
What job offer should you take?
Do you move for your spouse's job?
Do you have the surgery?
Do you move you mom to a nursing home?
Do you invest in your friend's business?
Do you loan your baby brother money?
Do you let your friend, uncle, or parent move in with you?

What two important decisions are you now facing?

1. _____

2. _____

"Life is the sum of all your choices."

- Camus

The purpose of this chapter is to learn a six-step decision-making process which will help you make better decisions – more thoughtful decisions.

Step #1 – List all the Pros and Cons of a Decision

Let's focus on the fundamental fact that most decisions have many potential consequences, results, or impacts. Very few important decisions in life are clear-cut or easy. The first thing you must do is to recognize that most decisions have both positive and negative impacts – pros and cons. The reality is that every major decision will have positive and negative impacts, pros and cons, upsides and downsides.

A lot of people get fixated or blinded by only one side of the decision, either the good impacts or the bad impacts. What you have to do is evaluate both the good and the bad.

You have to learn to see both the good and the bad of each decision clearly, objectively and non-emotionally.

A good beginning step is just to list the positives/negatives or pros/cons of the decision or choice.

Think about the impact of every decision on the six parts of your life - work, play, family, relationships, community, and spiritual.

EXAMPLE #1

DECISION:
I have a new job offer. What are the pros/cons of accepting that job offer versus staying at my current job?

PROS OF NEW JOB	CONS OF NEW JOB
More money	Longer hours
Flex time	Highly competitive industry-more risk
Better/more perks	More travel
New employer is financially more stable	No corporate childcare
	No education reimbursement
	Not a family-friendly environment
	Atmosphere is more political

EXAMPLE #2

DECISION:
Your spouse wants a bigger home in a different suburb.
Compared to your present home, the new home has the following
pros/cons:

PROS OF NEW HOME	CONS OF NEW HOME
More space	Larger mortgage
Closer to a better school	We need more furniture
Safer neighborhood	Snobbier neighbors
	Longer commute to my work
	Not as close to our family and friends

Listing the pros/cons helps you learn to think about the probable
consequences - advantages and disadvantages of the choices.

Let's list the pros and cons of your two decisions:
Think about the six parts of your life.

DECISION #1 -

PROS

A)_____

B)_____

C)_____

D)_____

E)_____

F)_____

CONS

A)_____

B)_____

C)_____

D)_____

E)_____

F)_____

DECISION #2 -

PROS

A)_____

B)_____

C)_____

D)_____

E)_____

F)_____

CONS

A)_____

B)_____

C)_____

D)_____

E)_____

F)_____

Step #2: Ranking Of Pros and Cons Based On Your Values and Goals

You have thought about the various pros/cons. Now, you have to rank them in order of importance based on your values and goals.

It should all be coming together for you. Your goals, objectives, and values prioritize not only your daily actions but also your daily choices and decisions.

My example #1: In determining whether to change jobs, you considered money, time, perks, flexibility, travel, commute time, childcare, educational tuition reimbursement, work atmosphere, and people.

Now rank them in order of importance to you based on your values and goals. The most important is number 1, the second is number 2, and so on. For example:

1. More money
2. Flex time
3. No travel
4. Childcare
5. Commute time

Step #3 – Create a Decision Matrix

DECISION MATRIX

Example:

Key Decision Factors (In Order of Priority)	Current Job (Choice A)	New Job (Choice B)
1. Money	_____	_____
2. Flex Time	_____	_____
3. Limited Travel	_____	_____
4. Childcare	_____	_____
5. Commute Time	_____	_____

For each factor think about the impact of choice A (current job) versus choice B (new job). Whichever alternative best fits or best meets the requirements of the key factor receives a #1, with the second choice a #2. If the alternatives are equal, each receives a 1 $\frac{1}{2}$.

Example:

Key Factor (Priority)	Current Job (Choice A)	New Job (Choice B)
Money (1)	2	1–More money
Flex Time (2)	1–More flex time	2
Limited Travel (3)	1–Less travel	2
Childcare (4)	1 $\frac{1}{2}$–(Equal)	1 $\frac{1}{2}$– (Equal)
Commute Time (5)	1–Shorter commute	2

Now, multiply the rank number of importance by the number result for each alternative and add up the totals.

Prior Example

Key Factor (Priority)	Current Job (Choice A)	New Job (Choice B)
Money (1)	X 2 = 2	X 1 = 1
Flex Time (2)	X 1 = 2	X 2 = 4
Limited Travel (3)	X 1 = 3	X 2 = 6
Childcare (4)	X 1 ½ = 6	X 1 ½ = 6
Commute Time (5)	X 1 = 5	X 2 = 10
TOTALS	**18**	**X 27**

The LOWEST total is the potential winner. The lowest total is some indication of a preference so far. The lowest total gives you some indication of the relative results based on your ranked values and objectives. It is critical to make sure you are honest about what is important to you – the rank of priorities.

Now, for your two key decisions let's weigh the pros and cons and create a decision matrix.

Remember, for each factor think about the impact of choice A versus choice B. Whichever alternative (A or B) best fits or best meets the requirements of the key factor receives a #1, with the second choice a #2. If the alternatives are equal, each receives a 1 ½. Once you have given each of the two choices a 1, 2, or 1 ½, multiply the rank number of importance by the number result for each alternative and add up the totals.

Most people get confused because it is the lowest number which gives you an indication of what your decision should be. To get reliable results, it is important to be honest in weighing the key factors. It is also critical for you to think hard about each factor and analyze each choice.

DECISION MATRIX FOR DECISION #1:

Your Key Decision Factors (In Order of Priority)	Choice A	Choice B
_____(1)	X__ = __	X__ = __
_____(2)	X__ = __	X__ = __
_____(3)	X__ = __	X__ = __
_____(4)	X__ = __	X__ = __
_____(5)	X__ = __	X__ = __
TOTALS	__	__

DECISION MATRIX FOR DECISION #2:

Your Key Decision Factors (In Order of Priority)	Choice A	Choice B
_____(1)	X__ = __	X__ = __
_____(2)	X__ = __	X__ = __
_____(3)	X__ = __	X__ = __
_____(4)	X__ = __	X__ = __
_____(5)	X__ = __	X__ = __
TOTALS	__	__

That is some indication of your assessment so far. But we still have 3 more steps to do.

Step #4: "In-Your-Heart Test"

Which alternative feels the best? Which choice are you the most comfortable with? Why? Is this a good reason or are you being insecure or afraid? Which is the best fit for you?

For your two decisions, now apply the subjective test by asking yourself these questions:

Which alternative feels the best?
Why?
Which is more you?
Which plays to your strengths?
Which helps you move in the direction that is right for you?
Which decision moves you toward more goals and directions?

Decision #1:

_____

_____

_____

_____

Decision #2:

_____

_____

_____

_____

Step #5: What Is The Downside? How Bad Will A Mistake Be? What Happens If I'm Wrong?

Okay, you have done the decision matrix test and the subjective test. Now you probably have a leading choice. STOP - Sit back. If you take this course of action, what is the downside?

What can go wrong? How likely is a mistake? How bad is a mistake? How bad is the bad?

If I'm wrong, the following bad things could occur:
1. _____
2. _____
3. _____
4. _____

Our job example - If my new job is not good for me, I will:
1. Have moved and left my friends and home;
2. Have lost money;
3. Have hurt my family and disrupted my kids' schooling;
4. Maybe lose money upon resale of a new home;
5. Not be able to go back to my old job.

These are significant downsides. They require that you think hard about your decision.

There are many significant bads in my example. You need to be sure of changing jobs. Changing jobs can require a move which is disruptive and puts you in a totally new place without friends. The job has to be better and the increased money significant.

> **"Decide which is the line of conduct that presents the fewest drawbacks and then follow it out as being the best one, because one never finds anything perfectly pure and immixed or exempt from danger."**
>
> *- Machiavelli*

For each of your two decisions, apply the downside test.

___ What is the likelihood of being wrong?

___ If you are wrong, what will be the bad consequences on each area of your life?

___ How bad is the bad?

___ What can be done to fix the bad or mitigate it?

Decision #1

The negative consequences on the six parts of my life are:

1. Work

    a. _____

    b. _____

2. Family

    a. _____

    b. _____

3. Play

    a. _____

    b. _____

4. Relationships

    a. _____

    b. _____

5. Spirituality

    a. _____

    b. _____

6. Community

    a. _____

    b. _____

What is the likelihood of a bad? Now, how bad is the bad? Go back to your decision matrix and to your subjective test. Now, reevaluate your decision. Are you still comfortable?

Decision #2

The bad consequences on the six parts of my life are:

1. Work
   a. _____
   b. _____
2. Family
   a. _____
   b. _____
3. Play
   a. _____
   b. _____
4. Relationships
   a. _____
   b. _____
5. Spirituality
   a. _____
   b. _____
6. Community
   a. _____
   b. _____

What is the likelihood of a bad? Now, how bad is the bad? Go back to your decision matrix and to your subjective test. Now, reevaluate your decision. Are you still comfortable?

Step #6: Which Course Of Action Results In More Future Options, Or More Future Alternatives, Or More Flexibility For The Future?

We are living in a hyper-changing world. Which choice or decision maximizes your options for the future? Which gives you more flexibility for the future?

This last exercise requires you to ask the following questions:

- Which decision gives me the most flexibility or the most options going forward?
- Which decision has more flexibility if I'm wrong?
- Which decision "opens more doors" for me?
- Which decision gives me more choices in the future?
- Which decision will create more opportunities for me?

New Example: Job "A" versus Job "B"

You have a choice of two jobs. Job "A" requires you to move to a small town with few other employers. This small town is 40 miles from any larger town. Job "B" is in a larger city with many job alternatives. Well, if Job "A" was a mistake, or if Job "A" was the right choice and employer "A" went out of business or closed the plant or was bought by a competitor and consolidated, what would you do? Where would you find the next job? How would you afford to move back to your prior location? What disruptions would occur for the kids?

No one is ever 100% sure of what the right decision is. There are a lot of close calls in life. Always think about maximizing future options or alternatives if you make the wrong decision. Even if you make the right decision, events beyond your control can negatively impact the result. So again, focus on flexibility, keeping your options open, giving yourself alternatives.

For each of the two key decisions ask yourself these questions:

1. What choice gives me the most flexibility or options going forward? Why?
2. What choice gives me more flexibility if I'm wrong? Why?
3. Which decision or alternative "opens more doors" for me?

Decision #1

_____

_____

_____

_____

Decision #2

_____

_____

_____

_____

Let's review. In making decisions there is a six-step process of making a decision.
1. List all the pros/cons;
2. Rank the pros/cons by order of importance based on your goals and values;
3. Do a decision matrix;
4. Subjective in-your-heart test;
5. Downside evaluation – how bad is the bad?
6. Future options – what decision maximizes your future flexibility and options?

Remember the key words:
1. What are the pros/cons?
2. Rank them by your values and goals;
3. Do a matrix;
4. What's your heart say?
5. Downside evaluation;
6. Maximize future options.

Say them again:

1. What are the pros/cons?
2. Rank them by my values and goals;
3. Do a matrix;
4. What's my heart say?
5. Downside evaluation;
6. Maximize future options.

Lastly, for important decisions, seek advice from people you respect. Get input.

Make your decisions. To achieve your goals, you must make choices and decisions. Think and then decide. Decide and then act. MAKE IT HAPPEN!

Cut your losses.

If you make a bad decision, take your time and think through the alternatives. Go through the six-step process. Again, look to maximize future possibilities of achieving your goals and objectives. Admit the mistake, learn from it, and go on. Move forward.

Everyone makes mistakes. The only people who do not make mistakes are dead. Accept your mistakes and move on. Learn from them. Just don't make the same mistake twice.

Good decision making is a learned task. It is thinking through a problem or dilemma. Follow the six steps. Minimize big downsides and maximize future options and flexibility. Be true to your values and goals.

Well, what is your decision?

	Your Decision #1	**Your Decision #2**
Your Matrix:	_____	_____
In-Your-Heart Test:	_____	_____
Downside Test:	_____	_____
Future Options:	_____	_____
Final Conclusion:	_____	_____

CHAPTER NINE CONCLUSIONS

YOUR DECISION PROCESS

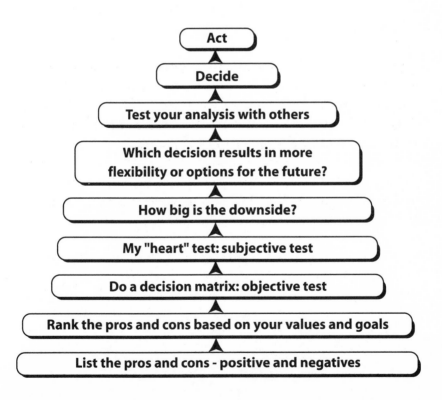

L earning and continual improvement is also key to you achieving your life-long goals and objectives.

Successful businesses cannot become complacent or arrogant. There is always room for improvement. Successful businesses strive for perfection, for zero errors, and continuously make small step-by-step improvements in their products and services.

You must do the same thing in your work life and in your personal life. Good jobs are very competitive. There is always someone trying to move up. You are competing every day to keep your current job and to move up to more money, more responsibility, etc. To stay in the game and to compete, what do you have to do?

In the new global competitive environment, your only security is your skills and your ability to learn.

Why should someone hire you? What value can you add? To compete in this environment you must (1) keep improving your skills and (2) learn new skills.

Once you accept this reality, it will cause you to look at your life differently. What opportunities do I have to learn? What opportunities do I have to get more education and training? Am I growing? Or am I stuck? Am I moving forward or standing still? What can I learn at this job to add to my list of skills? A good job gives you more than money; it gives you the opportunity to learn and to grow. Good employers help you learn.

It is very simple. If you cannot improve or learn new skills at your current job, you should consider finding a job that will give you the opportunity to learn. Ask for training, ask to learn new skills, push for being better.

If you cannot learn on the job, learn at home. Take courses, read books, seek out learning experiences. Do not let your current job hold you back.

You have to take ownership of your life. You have the responsibility to learn and to make yourself the best person you can be.

Everyone who wants to achieve more must also be able to market themselves and their knowledge or skills. Most people are timid about marketing themselves. If you don't - who will? To market yourself you must be able to communicate clearly and concisely.

Can you:
1. Write and express yourself in clear, concise sentences?
2. Speak clearly and confidently in business situations?
3. Market yourself confidently?
4. Project an image of being competent, secure, and confident – someone to rely on and trust?
5. Understand and deal with people of different backgrounds?
6. Use the computer, e-mail, internet, do basic research on the computer?
7. Understand basic numbers, and read business reports?
8. Manage your time efficiently?
9. Present a pleasing friendly image?

Do you keep up with events in the world, your town, and your employer?

Different jobs require different skills. Ask your boss what skills you need to improve or learn in order to advance. Go back to your strengths and weaknesses analysis. What did you need to learn or improve? What will you do about it? Again, Management by Objectives ("MBO"). What learning time do you set aside each week and do you measure your improvement?

In my current work position as a Team Leader, I ask my people each day to ask themselves two questions:

1. Did you do everything you could do today to be the best you can be?

And

2. Did you do everything you could today to help your team accomplish its goals?

THE LEARNING CIRCLE

Learning

Produces good feelings about yourself

Which gives you more self-confidence

Which gives you the courage to seek more opportunities to learn

"Luck is what happens when preparation meets opportunity."

- Darrell Royal

Learning feels good. Learning should make you feel proud of yourself and more self-confident. Self-confident people are able to seek out new experiences and more learning because they believe they can handle the new experiences.

Remember your objectives – what did you need to learn or improve on to meet your goals and objectives? What did you learn today?

What is your learning objective this week?

What is your learning goal for this month?

Set learning goals, measure your learning progress. Do it!

No matter how successful you are, if you are not learning, you are losing your edge.

Learn or lose!

LEARNING FEEDBACK LOOPS

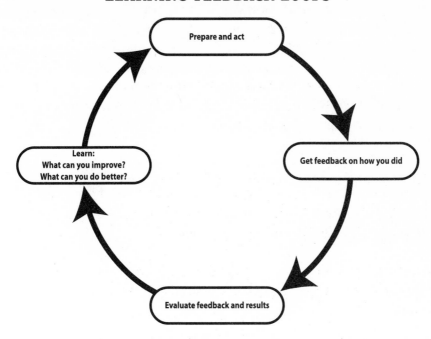

By living a proactive, can-do lifestyle where you try to take more control over your life, you will take actions, take steps, do things. What are the results of your actions? What is the feedback? What can you learn?

To be successful you have to:

1. Listen for and seek the feedback from your environment as to your actions;
2. Understand the feedback and evaluate the source of the feedback;
3. Accept good faith, well-intended critique, or constructive criticism;
4. Improve, learn, and keep moving toward your objectives and goals.

It may help to think about your life this way. By utilizing MBO every day, you have set forth your "to do" list. You are going out into the world and taking action to get done what you want. Your world, your environment involves people, organizations, whose goals and objectives are not the same as yours. Conflicts or frustrations will arise. It is natural. Okay, so you need to listen and hear the feedback, decide which feedback is important to you and adjust, adapt, learn, and keep on going.

The world will generally give you two types of feedback – positive or negative.

Positive Feedback

We all love to be told we are good, and to hear we did a good job. We all want to be loved and admired by someone. Positive feedback is good, but do not let it "go to your head" and do not become complacent, arrogant, or too self-confident.

When your boss, customer or client gives you positive feedback, thank them; but ask them what you can do to continue to improve, what can you do to help your customer or client more?

If you do not get feedback frequently from your supervisor, ask for it. Ask what am I dong wrong? What am I not doing that you want me to do? How can I keep learning? Seek out feedback. You need it. It helps you focus on what you need to do. It minimizes surprises.

Negative Feedback

Negative feedback is harder to deal with. Your first tendency will be to defend your actions and try to prove the person wrong. Sometimes this works, but most of the time it does not.

First, make sure you understand what is wrong. Get to the real issue. Most people are not totally direct or honest when they give you negative feedback because they are scared of hurting your feelings. Well, this does you no good. Try to get to the bottom of it.

To improve or correct the mistake, you MUST know what to correct. So keep asking for details, examples until you get a response you understand.

But do not stop here. Work out with the customer, supervisor, spouse, or friend a response or action which, if taken by you, may remedy or correct the problem or issue.

If that is not possible, make sure you understand what to do the next time a similar event occurs.

Negative Feedback – Always Consider The Source

One of my mentors, Ed Kessler, Head Offensive Football Coach at the University of Florida, told me something in 1967 that turned out to be one of those golden nuggets of truth for life:

"Always consider the source of negative feedback and their motivations."

Always try to understand whether the person has your best interests at heart or are they insecure, jealous of you, see you as competition, or as a threat to them. Understand where people are coming from and evaluate negative feedback accordingly.

Chapter Ten Conclusions

1. To win in the game of life you have to continually improve and continually learn.

2. Manage your learning process using MBO.

3. Set learning objectives and measure your results.

4. Learning produces good feelings and self-confidence which gives you the courage to seek out more learning.

5. Seek feedback. Learn from your experiences.

Make it Happen!

<u>Your Workspace</u>

A learning tool – mental rehearsal. Prepare, prepare, and prepare.

People learn in different ways. Some learn best by reading, some by listening, some by seeing, some by doing. Figure out your best way to receive, understand, and learn new information. Whatever way you learn best – use it. One learning aid that a lot of successful people utilize frequently is mental rehearsal.

Example:
Before a meeting or phone call, ask yourself the following questions:

1. What is the purpose of the meeting or call?
2. What do you want to accomplish?
3. What do you think the other person wants to accomplish?

REHEARSE in your mind what you will say or do. If it helps, write down an outline to use as a checklist.

REHEARSE in your mind the other person's possible responses. Think how you will respond to those responses. Visualize the interaction. Think about your answers to the difficult questions. Prepare yourself for the unexpected. How will you respond to surprising responses? What questions will be likely asked of you by the other person? What will be your response?

REHEARSE and go over in your mind – visualize - what may happen. Use your eyes and **VISUALIZE** it. Think about how you would respond to unexpected responses such as rudeness, yelling, arrogance, confrontation, or abruptly ending the call or the meeting.

Mental rehearsal should become a daily habit. It is a great tool. I use it every day to prepare for meetings, phone calls. It helps you be prepared. Preparation is where hard work meets opportunity. By being mentally prepared, you will have more self-confidence. You will exude confidence and security. People will feel your presence.

Mental rehearsal helps you to:
1. Focus on your objectives;
2. Be prepared;
3. React to the unexpected events appropriately;
4. Have self-confidence.

Mental Rehearsal Exercise

Tomorrow you have a call, a meeting, an important interaction with someone. Let's prepare for it using mental rehearsal.

1. Event:

   _____

2. What do you want to accomplish?
   a. _____
   b. _____
   c. _____

3. What do you think the other person wants to accomplish?
   a. _____
   b. _____
   c. _____

4. Who will speak first?

   _____

5. What will you say?

   _____

6. What do you expect the other person(s) to say?

_____

7. What objections, issues, or concerns might they raise?

_____

_____

_____

8. What are your answers to each of those possible objectives, issues, or concerns?

_____

_____

_____

9. What will you do if you do not meet your objectives?

_____

_____

10. What if the event is abruptly ended? How will you act?

_____

11. What if the event ends quicker than you expected it to?

_____

12. What if the person asks you why you want to do it?

_____

13. Why do you believe your position is right?

_____

14. Other possible questions you might want to consider in preparation for event:

_____

_____

_____

15. How will you act if the interaction is not favorable?

_____

_____

_____

Mental rehearsal can become second nature. When you first use it to prepare, I recommend that you write down your objectives. Write down key points. Write down key code words like, "be calm" or "be professional" or "be cool." After doing this for some time, you will do it naturally. Mental rehearsal keeps you moving toward your goals. Preparation leads to success.

One other key point. Interactions are like ball games. The momentum changes: Once you have accomplished your objectives, end the interaction as quickly as possible. Don't give the other person time to change the momentum.

A Learning Tool – Mental Replay

Just like mental rehearsal helps you prepare for events, a mental replay of an event helps you to learn from the event. Think about the meeting, phone call, and what you could have done better. What could you have done differently to increase your chance of achieving your objectives? How successful were you in achieving your objectives? What happened that caught you by surprise? What could you have done better?

Today, you had a meeting, call, or interaction which was important. Let us mentally replay it.

ACTION/OCCURRENCE

_____

My meeting objectives were: _____

_____

_____

The results were: _____

_____

_____

1. What happened that I was not prepared for?

_____

_____

2. What could I have done better?

_____

_____

3. How could I have achieved more of my objectives?

_____

_____

4. What did I learn?

_____

_____

5. If I had to do it all over again, what would I do differently?

_____

_____

Mental replay is as important as mental rehearsal. Mental replay is replaying in your mind key events, meetings, or occurrences. What could you have done better? What would you have done differently? What will you do differently next time? Mental replay helps you learn to listen and read people. A key to being a proactive impact player is listening as much as you talk. Focus on really hearing the other side's viewpoint and deal with it directly. Mental rehearsal and mental replay are vital success tools.

Chapter Eleven Conclusions

Mental Rehearsal –Mental Replay

1. Prepare for every key interaction.

2. Think about your objectives.

3. Rehearse the interaction in your mind.

4. Play what if's: What if he or she says this or that?

5. Good preparation gives you self-confidence.

6. As importantly, mentally replay your performance and critique your performance.

7. What could you have done better? What did you learn? What will you do differently next time?

Make it Happen!

<u>Your Workspace</u>

Chapter Twelve   What Else I Have Learned

I have been fortunate to have learned from and worked with some wonderful and successful people and businesses. I have spent a large portion of my career learning why some people or businesses succeed and why others do not.

Success or failure does not depend on native intelligence but more on attitude, approach, process, and people skills. The purpose of this book was to share with you what I have learned and what works.

The six success tools discussed in this book will give you a framework of how to do it – how to organize your life – how to allocate your time – how to make better decisions – how to find your strategic fit – how to prepare for meetings – and how to mentally replay and learn from your actions.

I believe these processes can be utilized by individuals to gain more control over their lives in a fast-paced, changing world. If you find Make It Happen! helpful, pass on these tools to your friends and to your children.

People who feel like they are accomplishing something each day will be happier, more self-confident, and more successful. The more people who feel this way, the better place this world will be.

Live it daily! Make It Happen!

We have learned how to apply the tools of strategic fit, MBO, chunking, risk/reward decision making, mental rehearsal, and mental replay learning to your life. These principles are tools to incorporate into how you live your life on a daily basis.

Remember that to achieve your goals and objectives you must have both a daily positive can-do attitude and a daily proactive action plan. A positive, proactive, can-do attitude is critical to having staying power, overcoming life's defeats, setbacks, and annoyances which we all will suffer.

But to live life proactively, you must act - make something happen. Strategic analysis, MBO prioritization, focus and measurement, decision analysis, learning by mental rehearsal and mental replay are tools, aids, processes that you can learn from, adopt, and incorporate into your life on a daily basis to manage your life.

Have you made your daily to-do list on your 3x5 index card today?

So let's move on - to what else I have learned.

1. Mentoring

Most successful people in business have a mentor or sponsor. Someone to learn from, someone to seek advice from, someone who can be counted on to give constructive, objective advice.

One of your goals or objectives should be to identify and build one or two strategic helping relationships or friendships with people who will help you achieve your objectives. People who will take your best interests to heart and not seek to profit from or use confidential information to your detriment. This is hard to do. But it can be done.

> **"Keep away from people who try to belittle your ambitions. Small people always do that, but the really great make you feel that you, too, can become great."**
>
> *- Mark Twain*

How do you identify mentors in your work world?

Every organization has a few people who are successful and get a lot of emotional satisfaction and joy from helping other people grow and advance. Who are these people? Look for evidence or a track record of mentoring. Who promotes the most people? Who helps people move into other departments? Who suggests ways to succeed or improve? Who is known as a "straight shooter" and as a fair person? Who has morals and integrity and does not use his or her position of power to intimidate people or harass people?

Do your homework, figure out who could be a good mentor. In the beginning, seek out their advice. Go slow.

VERY IMPORTANT POINTS FOR WOMEN:

Finding a mentor is harder for you because there are fewer women managers and supervisors. You may have to seek out a male mentor. Make sure you are crystal clear in that you are only looking for good business or career advice. Find a mentor who has a good track record of helping women advance without demanding anything in return. Find a mentor who has daughters that are a success. Beware of single mentors.

Do not put yourself in situations that may send the wrong signal. Meet at lunch hour – not after work. Seek out advice at work – not outside of work.

Remember, most companies have rules against fraternization between supervisor and employee. But if it occurs, it is usually the woman employee who leaves – not the boss. Do not mix work and pleasure.

Understand that good mentors like to mentor. They get a lot of satisfaction from helping people. Good mentors are always consciously or subconsciously looking for their next student or mentor. **Good mentors and good mentees need each other.**

What are mentors looking for in a mentee?

Mentors are looking for people with the right attitude and with the potential to grow and make progress. Mentors are looking for people who project a desire to learn, a commitment to excellence, a willingness to work hard and learn. Mentors are looking for potential winners.

What image do you project – secure or insecure? Enthusiastic or just going through the motions? A person who has pride in himself or herself?

Stop. Think about how you come across. What is your image? Do people like being around you? Are you a positive person or a "downer"? People generally fall into one of two camps - those who see the glass as half full and those who see the glass as half empty. Be a person who sees the glass as half full and project enthusiasm, determination and stand for excellence, quality and honesty.

How do you start to build a mentor relationship?

Research and seek out the right mentor and ask for advice on how to grow and succeed in the business environment. Start slow, ask only a few questions. Go off and perform. The mentor will be watching to determine whether you are a player worth coaching.

Once you have made some progress, if the mentor does not seek you out, seek him or her out and report back. Ask for more advice. Building a mentor relationship takes time.

Be Selective.

The corollary to seeking out and developing mentoring relationships at work and friendships in your personal life is to continually evaluate your network and always be willing to upgrade your network. Yes, you should be loyal to your friends. But you should make sure you are getting something out of those relationships which helps you accomplish your goals and objectives in one or more of the six compartments of life – work, play, family, relationships, community, and spiritual.

You only have so much time and energy. You have to protect your time and emotional energy. Be selective where you spend it and critique your emotional returns.

The Mentor/Mentee Code

Good mentors ask for nothing in return. "Thank you's" should be plentiful and sincere. However, if you are fortunate to have a good mentor, the "unwritten law" is that you have the duty to be someone else's mentor.

One way of paying back a mentor is to help someone else. Pass on what you have learned; pass on the good advice to a good "mentee."

In writing this book, there were some other important lessons which I have learned and which I felt had to have a small place in our journey together. That is what follows.

You see, I have been lucky and fortunate. To help you achieve more is my mission now. Godspeed and Good Luck.

2. I'm Too Tired

Daily Positive Can-Do Attitude + Daily Positive Action = Success
A proactive lifestyle requires a positive "can-do" daily attitude
and an actively managed life using the tools which we have
discussed. Some days you will be tired and just want to
coast. You're tired of being psyched-up and going for it each day.
I understand. I've been there, too. How do you deal with those
feelings? First, you never know what lucky break or opportunity
will present itself on any given day. Bottom line, you have to be
ready to play.

When you go to work you need to have on your game face.
**Sometimes you just have to kick yourself in the butt
and just do it.** That is what separates the professionals from
the amateurs, the players from the "wannabes." Learn to recharge
yourself on your off days. Find out what relaxes you and allows
you to really rest. Plan your playtime doing what rejuvenates you
on your off days. It is okay to rest and recharge but do it at the
right time. Whatever that is – exercise, gardening, reading,
cooking, sewing, knitting, etc. Treasure and allocate yourself a
chunk of time to recharge. Protect your "you time."

Each day, allow yourself 20 minutes of "you time" when you are
alone, and you can rest, and not "be on." Use coffee breaks or
lunch breaks to "get away." Yes, you will get tired. But play to
win every time you take the field in the game of life.

3. I'm Anxious – I'm Scared

Most people want to do good. Most people want to be successful. Some people just do not know how to do it. That is what this book is about – six tools for success.

Other people are paralyzed by being afraid of trying; they do not want to fail; they do not want to look stupid. They do not have the self-confidence to act.

Everyone is anxious. Everyone gets scared. Being anxious and scared and having butterflies is natural. But you do have a choice as to how you react to these feelings. These feelings can paralyze you, make you procrastinate, be inactive, and cause you to make excuses about why you did not succeed. Or, you can accept the feelings and prepare to take action using the mental rehearsal tool and build your self-confidence and act.

Nike had the right idea when they said, "Just do it" as did Woody Allen when he said, "85% of life is showing up." It's not that hard. Try. Make It Happen!. Prepare yourself and take small steps.

> **"If you want to conquer fear, don't sit at home and think about it. Go out and get busy."**
>
> *- Dale Carnegie*

4. Working Hard is a Given

You were probably surprised because nowhere in the preceding 213 pages have we talked about working hard. Why? Because it is a given. You know that to accomplish your goals and be good at what you do in any area of your life requires hard work.

5. Life Gets Easier As You Get Older – NOT SO!

The world is changing at a faster pace. The work world is more competitive today than when I started in 1971. I work harder and thankfully, smarter today than I did then. In today's world, advantages or leads evaporate quickly because information is so readily available and quickly transmitted to everyone.

To achieve your goals and objectives takes a lifelong plan of learning and actively managing your life to achieve your goals.

6. Life Is Precarious – You Never Know When Your Number Will Be Up

Today may be my or your last day on this earth. Did you take care of any unfinished personal business? Did you say "thank you" and "I love you" to the VIPs in your life? It could be their last conversation with you and memory of you.

7. The Truth Will Come Out

You will make mistakes. It is far easier to admit mistakes than to cover them up or lie. In the business world mistakes are a given. Tell your supervisor quickly and directly and state what corrective action you have taken or can take.

Do not let an unhappy client or customer catch your supervisor off guard. Give your supervisor a "heads up." Prepare him or her for the angry customer or client.

Be a stand-up player and admit you made a mistake. Say "I'm sorry" and "I learned from it" and then move on. That's life.

If someone asks you a question and you don't know the answer, say that you don't know but that you will get them the answer. Be honest.

8. Be Humble – Most People Will Forget About You Within Three Days After You Die

Keep yourself and your importance in perspective. Most of us do not save lives or impact world peace or salvation. Arrogance, conceit, and putting down the less fortunate or the less lucky is wrong. Likewise, do not blame others for your shortcomings and do not look for racial, religious, or ethnic scapegoats. Basically all human beings are alike and we are all trying to make something out of our lives. We all have the same fears, hopes, and dreams. Yes, we are all God's children.

9. Values Are What's Really Important

Your world will change. Your relationships will change. Your spouse will change. We are all evolving stories. Your life is one giant soap opera. Your job will change. So what is the foundation, the glue that holds your life together or that gives you some consistency or stability?

Your values. Your values are what you stand for. Your values are the bedrock of your life. Values are the guideposts to help you do what is right. Your values are what you live by.

What values are most important to you? Love, courage, honesty, loyalty, helping others, justice, individual freedom, equality? What does and will your life stand for?

A person without values is like a car without a steering wheel – a boat without a rudder. What helps give your life direction and meaning are values that you believe in and act on.

10. The Real Killer of Life's Spirit is Hopelessness

A can-do attitude and a daily to-do list with specific chunk bite-size tasks should give you the feeling of accomplishment and movement toward what is important to you. Fight hopelessness and despair with small steps toward your mountaintop. There will be bad times, but bounce back.

11. The Most Under-Appreciated and Underutilized Resources in This World are Women.

12. God grant me the serenity to accept the things I cannot change; the courage to change the things I can; and the wisdom to know the difference.

13. Perseverance Is a Key to Success.

Most people give up too easily. But be aware that there is a fine line between perseverance and stupidity. Know when to cut your losses.

14. Life is ambiguity and change.

15. Successful People Should Be Kind People, Too

Treat children and animals kindly. Treat the less fortunate and the less lucky kindly.

16. The Unknown

You will find yourself in situations that are new and that are scary. Take a deep breath and go back to basics. First, get the facts. Then learn the rules of the new game. Remember your values. Think. Analyze using your decision tools. Get advice. Then make a decision and act.

17. Be True to Yourself

Daily do things which affirm your being. I'm 52 years old and I still say my prayers daily. It is my time to reflect and give thanks and to be honest about how scary and uncertain life is. But it gives me strength and confidence to go on and strive to teach and try to help people.

<u>Your Workspace</u>

MAKE IT HAPPEN!
Your Conclusions

	Yes	No
I want to take more ownership of my life.		
I want to have more control over my life.		
I want to achieve more of my goals.		
I want to feel happier and be more successful.		
I can do it.		
I will do it.		
I will work at it daily.		
I will have a positive can-do attitude daily.		
I understand that I have to have my own game plan.		
I have to understand my strengths and weaknesses.		
I have to be smart and take into account my environment.		
I have to find my strategic fit – where my strengths can flourish.		
I need to prioritize my goals.		
I need to focus daily on taking small steps toward my goals.		
I need to manage my time daily.		
I need to make better decisions.		
I need to prepare by mental rehearsal.		
I need to critique myself by mental replay.		
I need to have the courage to try.		
I need to make something happen daily.		

	Yes	No
I need to:		
Priority		
Focus		
Act		
Learn from feedback		
I need to make better decisions by focusing on:		
All the pros/cons		
Setting values to the decision factors and doing a decision matrix		
Minimizing the downside risk; and Maximizing future actions and alternatives		
I will prepare using mental rehearsal.		
I will learn using mental replay.		

What we have learned together is a process of how to live life more proactively and with a defined, can-do, proactive attitude.

Good Luck!

Godspeed!

FEEDBACK REQUEST

I want your feedback. What worked for you? What issues or problems did you have with my approach? What advice would you give me to make this book more helpful to you?

Please send your comments to:

edhess@makeithappen.net

Or fax your comments to me at:

(770) 980-2026

APPENDIX: Quotes

<u>You are your answer</u>

1.   "Nothing can bring you peace but yourself."

                                        - Ralph Waldo Emerson

2.   "Happiness depends upon ourselves."

                                          - Aristotle

3.   "The man who makes everything that leads to happiness depend upon himself and not upon other men, has adapted the best plan for living happily."

                                          - Plato

<u>To be at peace with yourself</u>

4.   "Happiness is when what you think, what you say, and what you do are in harmony."

                                          - Gandhi

Be proactive

5.   **"People are always blaming their circumstances for what they are. The people who get on in this world are those who get up and look for circumstances they want, and if they can't find them, make them."**

- George Bernard Shaw

6.   **"A life of reaction is a life of slavery, intellectually and spiritually. One must fight for a life of action, not reaction."**

- Rita Mae Brown

7.   **"A wise man will make more opportunities than he find."**

- Frances Bacon

Attitude

8.   **"The greatest discovery of my generation is that man can alter his life by simply altering his attitude of mind."**

- William James

9.   **"The last of the human freedoms: to choose one's attitude in any given set of circumstances, to choose one's own way."**

- Victor Frankel

Decisions

10.   "Life is the sum of all your choices."

- Camus

11.   "Decide which is the line of conduct that presents the fewest drawbacks and then follow it out as being the best one, because one never finds anything perfectly pure and immixed or exempt from danger."

- Machiavelli

Finding your answer

12.   "What's important is finding what works for you."

- Henry Moore

Act–Make it happen

13.   "If you want to conquer fear, don't sit at home and think about it. Go out and get busy."

- Dale Carnegie

14.   "To do is to be."

- Socrates

"To be is to do."

- Plato

15.   **"The only man who makes no mistakes is the man who never does anything."**
        - Eleanor Roosevelt

16.   **"Mean to don't pick no cotton."**
        - Anonymous

Chunking

17.   **"Nothing is particularly hard if you divide it into small jobs."**
        - Henry Ford

18.   **"Great things are not done by impulse, but by a series of small things brought together."**
        - Vincent van Gogh

19.   **"Little strokes fell great oaks."**
        - Benjamin Franklin

20.   **"Life is like that; one stitch at a time taken patiently, and the pattern will come out all right, like embroidery."**
        - Oliver Wendell Holmes

Change

21.   "There is nothing permanent except
       change."

                                    - Heraclitus

Success

22.   "Today is your day: Your mountain is
       waiting. So, get on your way!"

                                    - Dr. Seuss

Mentoring

23.   "Keep away from people who try to
       belittle your ambitions. Small people
       always do that, but the really great
       make you feel that you, too, can become
       great."

                                    - Mark Twain

Mental Rehearsal

24.   "Luck is what happens when
       preparation meets opportunity."

                                    - Darrell Royal